WORDS

TO DIE FOR

WORDS
TO DIE FOR

VERSES THAT SHAPED
THE LIVES OF 30 PEOPLE
WHO CHANGED THE WORLD

LAWRENCE KIMBROUGH

Nashville, Tennessee

WORDS TO DIE FOR

Copyright © 2002
Broadman & Holman Publishers • Nashville, Tennessee
ISBN 0-8054-3908-0
Printed in Belgium
All Rights Reserved

1 2 3 4 04 03 02

INTRODUCTION

If we all knew our church history a little better, we wouldn't feel like we were enduring Christian suffering every time the preacher's sermon ran a few minutes over.

We'd know better. We'd know that worship is a privilege. We'd know that our pews have been padded by men and women who served Christ when it hurt, when it cost them . . . when it killed them. We'd know them as real, flesh-and-blood people who could have taken the easy way but instead chose the high road. Faithful brothers and sisters who wouldn't give up, wouldn't back down, and—when ordered to stop—wouldn't take no for an answer.

We need to know them. And the Scriptures that inspired them.

For in getting to know them, we remind ourselves that we serve the same God, that we share the same faith in Christ, that the Bible we hold in our hands carries the same precious promises that compelled them to acts of uncommon courage, and that even in our own commonplace lives we can do what God has dreamed for us.

I have a lot to learn about church history. I know just enough, as the saying goes, to be dangerous. In fact, I probably shouldn't admit it, but I started this book knowing little more about these individuals than their given names. But now I've studied their lives, researched their biographies, read their writings. And I have been overwhelmed by what they did—and who they were.

So if anything you read in here is wrong, inconsistent, or outright offensive, I apologize. Honest mistakes. But if you find yourself moved by the accounts of these great heroes, commit yourself to rediscovering (as these men and women did) the power of God's Word, promising to remain in it every day, and as the Holy Spirit speaks through it, to go forth in His strength . . . to change your world.

Perhaps you can use these readings in your personal devotions. Or maybe share them in a church class or small group, using the articles as an introduction, the "What's Your Story?" section as points for discussion, and the related Scriptures as a Bible study base.

It's up to you. Whatever works best for you.

Now to roll the credits: I'd like to thank my friends Matt Price and Steve Keels for sharing their insights on these chapters and making me think. Thanks also to my pastor, Arch Warren, for helping me keep this book true to character—and for helping me keep my *life* true to character each week through your sermons and Christ-like example.

Thanks to all my buddies and coworkers at B&H for your Christian faith and friendship, especially David Shepherd and Ricky King for letting me take a crack at this, Diana Lawrence for making my writing look a lot better than it is, Vicki Lee and others for catching all my mistakes, Stephanie Huffman and Sam Gantt for their enthusiasm, Lloyd Mullens and the Bible Translation team for their extra work, the Sales folks for all their encouragement, and Kay Whitley for crunching the numbers and buying me some time.

The biggest thanks goes to my wife, Kim, for her very helpful yet always kind-hearted comments (you helped me give this book what it really needed), to my daughters, Carrie and Grace, for bringing me hugs and hot coffee, and to my parents and teachers who first introduced me to some of these world changers—and pointed me to Christ, the One who changes everything.

*"Their devotion inspires us not only by their example,
but because we should have the same."*
Blaise Pascal

contents

ATHANASIUS

In the beginning was the Word; and the Word was with God, and the Word was God. . . . The Word became flesh and took up residence among us. We observed His glory, the glory as the only Son from the Father, full of grace and truth.

—John 1:1, 14

AᵀHAⁿASίUS
AGAINST THE WORLD

ALEXANDRIA, EGYPT · 328

Perhaps you've never even heard his name. Join the club. For those of us who weren't schooled in church history—or at least weren't paying close enough attention—the name of Athanasius just doesn't carry the common knowledge weight of a Martin Luther or a Saint Augustine.

But the church today would be a different kind of place if not for a short, dark-skinned, red-bearded half-hermit who singlehandedly fought an empire for the truth of the gospel. For much of the fourth century A.D., it was *Athanasius contra mundum*—"Athanasius against the world."

And Athanasius won.

To some historians, his was a battle that caused more trouble than it was worth. In many respects, his argument hung on a pen mark that had little more grammatical value than the dot of an "i"—a slight difference in pronunciation. A hiccup. But imbedded in that slender distinction was the essence of Christian faith. And he would defend it with his life.

"We are contending," he wrote, "for our all."

Up until then, the church's major threats had all come from the outside—Roman emperors with the power to act on their suspicions and to legalize their cruelty, Greek philosophers more interested in asking questions than in seeking answers. Those who led God's people after the deaths of the apostles shed much ink—and much blood—defending the ideals and ideas of Christian faith against the heavy tide of a hostile and haughty world.

But by the early 300s, egos and ambitions had begun drawing battle lines *within* the church family, and brother was fighting brother over theological positions and doctrinal camps. Most of the differences formed around explanations of the Trinity: Did Christians serve one God, or three? Was the Father greater than the Son and Spirit, or equal? Was God unchangeable, or not?

And then around 318 came an upstart church leader named Arius, asking the question to rattle all questions: Was Jesus even God at all?

It was a controversy that not only occupied the studies of the scholars but also the bantered opinions of the millers and merchants, the travelers and townsfolk. It even reached the ears of Constantine (professing Christian and head of the Roman Empire), who called bishops from both East and West to an unprecedented gathering in the city of Nicea to set the record straight. When the two-month meeting finally broke in the late summer of 325, the resulting creed accurately declared Jesus Christ to be "very God of very God, begotten not made, of the same substance as the Father." Arius was declared a heretic, deposed and disgraced. And everyone assumed that the matter was closed.

Yet the issue continued to confuse and divide. Constantine, who probably valued the unity of his empire more than the truth of the gospel, ordered the new bishop of Alexandria to reinstate Arius as a member in good standing, a sharer in the church's communion.

But the new bishop was a man named Athanasius. And Athanasius told the emperor he could forget it.

"The Word of God came in His own person, because it was He alone, the Image of the Father, who could recreate man made after the image."

Assuming the legend is true, Athanasius stopped the emperor's parade through the streets one day, grabbed the ruler's horse by the bridle, and warned the great Constantine that these matters of Christian faith were even bigger than he was.

The consequences were that important. And this was why:

- If the Son was a created being, then the Son was not God.
- If the Son was not God, then God was not truly revealed in Him.
- If God was not truly revealed in Him, then the Son's death was worthless.

"The things which they, as men, rule out as impossible, He plainly shows to be possible; and things which these wiseacres laugh at as 'human,' He by His inherent might declares divine."

"For He alone," Athanasius said, "being Word of the Father and above all, was able to re-create all, and worthy to suffer on behalf of all and to be an ambassador for all with the Father. For this purpose the incorruptible Word of God entered our world.

"The Word is God from God; for 'the Word was God.'"

In other words, if Jesus is anything less than God—whether angel, or exalted teacher, or cosmic mediator—His death and resurrection cannot break the curse of sin. We can *say* that we're saved by His sacrifice, but in reality we're as lost as last year's Easter eggs.

Naturally, such defiant disobedience didn't go far in winning Athanasius friends at the palace. Constantine's mood toward the young bishop took such a hard turn for the worse that he banished him to the westernmost point in the empire, sending him miles away in mid-winter from Egypt to Gaul (modern France). It was the first of five exiles he would endure throughout his 45 years as bishop—a series of imperial temper tantrums that would cost him 17 years in hiding and on the run.

Once—in 356—the order of exile came not with the firm point of a royal finger but with the sharp point of a Roman sword. Soldiers surrounded the church at night as Athanasius led his congregation in worship. "The laity who remained with us cried out that we should seek our safety. I refused, saying that I would not leave until they were safely outside." But soon the crash of splintered wood and the flurry of drawn weapons shattered the solemn vigil. The monks and clergy picked up little Athanasius in their arms, carrying him to safety as the brazen general darted about the altar seeking to capture and kill the object of his mission.

Again, Athanasius was on his own, pushed toward the perimeters, wandering in the desert, living in caves, praying that those who could not defend their doctrines with Scripture would never be allowed to prevail with might.

The emperors would come and go—through both death and deceit. Athanasius would be allowed to return—always to the delight of his city. But the imperial pressure would eventually reheat, Athanasius would take his stand in the fire, and no one who denied the absolute divinity of Jesus Christ would find a minute's rest in his presence.

Yes, he admitted, the Incarnation was a mystery. No one could fully understand it. But there were those whose pride would not allow them not to know. And he would not keep silent while they robbed God of His power and the gospel of its truth. "We take divine Scripture, and set it up as a light upon its candlestick, saying: very Son of the Father, natural and genuine, proper to His essence, very and only Word of God is He. . . . But let them learn that 'the Word became flesh;' and let us, retaining the general scope of the faith, acknowledge that what they interpret ill, has a right interpretation."

Frantic world leaders, fearing a church split on their hands, sought a compromise in the wording of the Nicene creed to say that Christ was of "similar" instead of the "same substance" with the Father. The change in the Greek word was so small that one would hardly notice it. But to Athanasius it was the difference between life and death—for him, for the church, for the generations to come.

"God has made the true wisdom Itself to take flesh, and to become man, and to undergo the death of the cross; that by faith in Him, all that believe may obtain salvation. . . . Only so is our salvation fully realized and guaranteed."

He would die in 373 before the fruits of his labor would properly ripen. But at the Council of Constantinople in 381, the convening bishops would uphold his doctrine of the divinity of Christ. The Nicene creed would survive as the accepted understanding of the Trinity in the minds of most people of faith.

And the true church would proclaim a pure gospel to this day . . . because Athanasius had stood his ground. One man. Against the world.

WHAT'S YOUR STORY?

Athanasius lived at a time when people understood that beliefs had consequences. Doctrines were not unhinged from daily life but rather defined the way it looked. I know that getting a handle on what we believe takes time and work. But we cannot share with others what we don't know ourselves. Can you make a good case for the faith you profess? Ask God to show you how.

Deuteronomy 4:1-10 • John 16:12-15 • 2 Timothy 1:8-14

AUGUSTINE

Let us walk with decency, as in the day-
light; not in carousing and drunkenness;
not in sexual impurity and promiscuity;
not in quarreling and jealousy. But put
on the Lord Jesus Christ, and make no
plans to satisfy the fleshly desires.

—Romans 13:13-14

AUGUSTINE
TAKE AND READ

MILAN, ITALY · 386

Aurelius Augustinus—Milan's chief professor of rhetoric who could take your philosophical position apart and smash it into a thousand pieces before your very eyes.

He was now 31, and one of the most brilliant men in the Roman Empire.

But one day in August of the year 386, an unlikely visitor to his door and an unexplainable voice in his courtyard kicked out all the supports of his confidence and charisma, bringing him to the brink of despair, "going mad on my way to insanity."

The visitor was a man from Africa who held an important position in Italy's imperial court. He had stopped by Aurelius' house to talk, had noticed a copy of Paul's epistles lying on the reading table, and—assuming he was in Christian company—asked if Aurelius was familiar with the incredible sacrifices many were making for the cause of Christ. *No?* Why, two state officials the man knew personally had recently abandoned their jobs in response to their newfound faith. They and their fiancées had even decided to forsake marriage, dedicating their lives to God instead.

In days past Aurelius might have shrugged and snickered at such stories— decent people, throwing their lives away chasing foolish myths. But unexpectedly, pain began flushing its way across his face—not only from reaction to the man's reports, but from the torture of a troubled conscience that was thinking back half a lifetime. . . .

There Aurelius, a 16-year-old boy, sitting idle from school while his father saved enough money to send him to Carthage, was getting a different kind of education in the school of sexual freedom. Plunging headlong into promiscuity, he had "burned for all the satisfactions of hell," outperforming his friends in doing more, going farther, sinking lower. By the age of 18, fornication had made him a father with a woman he continued to keep as a mistress for another ten years or more.

But while wanton sin was claiming his body, his mind was falling in love with learning. Eagerness soon became eloquence; the student soon became the teacher. And bored with the Bible as a poor excuse for literature, he soon became an easy touch for a brand of religious mysticism that seemed more worthy of his scholastic skill. For the next nine years, while his intellectual pursuits were reaping rewards beyond measure, his spiritual pursuits were leading him from one twisted truth to the next.

Throughout his twenties, his life was a jumble of travel, triumphs, and troubles. From his hometown to Carthage, Carthage to Rome, Rome to Milan. He wrote two or three books, spent his free time in the gladiator arena and the theatre, and basked in the academic brotherhood of ideas. But he nearly lost his shirt in Rome when his rhetoric students refused to pay their fees, nearly lost his life to a sudden illness, and slowly lost even his awkward faith to the loopholes and inconsistencies of his adopted religion.

"I loved the happy life but I feared to find it in Your house, and so I ran from it even as I sought after it. I did not believe that a cure for this disease lay in Your mercy."

Yet through it all, one thing remained constant: Aurelius had a godly, praying mother named Monica.

He had broken her heart as a rebellious youth, but not her love. He had soiled her name, but nothing could stop her prayers. When her husband died, she followed Aurelius to Carthage, only to find him scorning God and embracing error. She begged the local bishop to talk to him. He too had once been a follower of the same religious sect as Aurelius. *I know he will listen to you!* No, the wise bishop answered. Aurelius must find out for himself. "Pray to the Lord that he will discover *by reading* what his error is." But be sure of this, the bishop said, as he looked deeply into Monica's weeping eyes: "It is impossible that the son of these tears should perish."

"There is one road, and only one, secured against all possibility of going astray, provided by One who is both God and man. As God He is the goal. As man He is the way. Apart from this way no one has been set free, no one is being set free, no one will be set free."

When her wayward son decided to leave for Rome, Monica ran down to the ship, refusing to let him leave without her. But by a trick, a lie, a full sail in the dead of night, he slipped her grasp and escaped the last tie to his childhood Christianity . . . until she showed up a year later in Milan, braving land and sea to witness the turning of his soul—a result she had seen in dreams and visions, a reward she knew by faith was only a matter of time. So on that day in 386 when Aurelius' African guest got up to leave, Aurelius' mother was likely in the kitchen or an upstairs bedroom, praying as she cooked and cleaned, waiting for the moment when God would get through.

She didn't have much longer to wait.

The stories his visitor had told him brought Aurelius' many accomplishments crashing down on his head, dispersing into a pile of meaningless rubble, and leaving him standing "naked in my own sight." The shame and sorrow drove him outside into his courtyard, under a fig tree at the bottom of his garden, and into a depth of uncontrollable weeping his once-proud soul had never known.

Then from somewhere he heard a voice. It seemed to be saying . . . somehow . . . "Take and read. Take and read." *Where was it coming from? From one of the other houses? From a nearby yard? An adjacent window?*

Gathering himself, he raced back into the house, snatched up the copy of Paul's letters he had left inside, "opened it, and in silence read the passage on which my eyes first fell"—Romans, chapter 13.

The thirteenth verse spoke of things he knew well—orgies, drunkenness, jealousy, anger. But the fourteenth verse spoke of one thing he had forgotten, if he had ever known it at all—that Jesus Christ was his only answer.

There was no need to read on.

"In that instant, with the very ending of the sentence, it was as though a light of utter confidence shone in my heart, and all the darkness of uncertainty vanished."

His mother danced. Aurelius' eyes filled yet again with tears. In his famous *Confessions*, he would write in praise to God: "Thou didst call, and cry, and burst my deafness. Thou didst gleam, and glow, and dispel my blindness. Thou didst touch me, and I burned for thy peace."

But while he would live to the age of 75 in the peace of forgiven sin, he would give his mortal life (almost unwillingly) to the uneasy life of the priesthood. The fourth and fifth-century church was fighting for its soul against the evil winds of falsehood and division. And no one would fight harder through the pen and the pulpit than Aurelius Augustinus, bishop of the North African city of Hippo.

Augustine.

In his massive book, *The City of God*, he would defend the Christians against those who blamed them for weakening Rome and making it ripe for collapse. He would argue against outright blasphemy in his major work *On the Trinity*. He would defend the doctrines of Scripture against the most invasive threats of the day.

And in the face of often hostile opposition and personal threats, he would set the tone for Western theology and thinking for centuries.

Finally, with his city squeezed in the merciless grip of homeland traitors and foreign thugs, he found on his deathbed the quiet rest he had so long desired. "The seventh day," he had said, "is without evening; it has no sunset."

But it did have a praying mother—and a loving Father—who knew that "by reading" he would find his way home.

WHAT'S YOUR STORY?

You can run but you can't hide. You can seek your satisfaction in sin or soak it in pleasures and laziness. You can milk your own self-importance for more than it's worth. But all you'll have to show for it is a deeper hole of disappointments. If you want to find a place to really relax, a place to rest in the middle of a crazy world, "take and read"—and enjoy the satisfying pleasure of God's presence.

Psalm 23:1-6 • Matthew 11:28-30 • 2 Timothy 3:1-17

JOHANN SEBASTIAN BACH

The trumpeters and singers resounded together, with one voice, to praise and thank the Lord. . . . The temple, the Lord's temple, was filled with a cloud. . . . for the glory of the Lord filled God's temple.

—2 Chronicles 5:13-14

JOHANN
SEBASTIAN BACH
GLORY TO GOD

LEIPZIG, GERMANY · 1733

J. S. Bach may seem an odd fit for a book like this.

He was a musician, not a martyr. An organist, not an antagonist. A composer, not a reformer. He lived and worked in a time of relative peace in his homeland, two centuries after Martin Luther had exposed the dry rot of official German religion. By the 1700s most of the dust from that historic battle had settled into fairly neat piles, and a job as choir director in the Lutheran church had become a mark of distinction, not derision.

So, no—the verse God used to inspire Bach's service never came close to putting him on the run or at enemy gunpoint. He was never in the slightest danger of being burned at the stake. Instead the Word lit a fire that burned *inside him*—a passion so intent on honoring God through music that it kept him awake into the night, raining melodies onto the page, his hands having to work fast to keep pace with his mind.

It had started young. His whole family, actually, had been creators and performers of music for as far back as anyone could remember. In fact, their family name had become so synonymous with music that any musician living in their hometown of Eisenach was often called . . . a "Bach."

But he had been orphaned at age ten, and an older brother (Christoph) had taken him into his home, assuming full responsibility for keeping the family legacy alive. He taught his little brother as much as he felt he was ready for. But the young Bach easily mastered all the pieces set before him . . . and hungered for more. So at night he would creep to the cabinet where Christoph kept a book of piano music written by the great masters of the day, reach his small hand through the grillwork, and roll the book just tightly enough to slip it through without notice. For six months he continued this secret capture, copying the book by moonlight, then returning it to its place, only to be caught by his brother one night and forced to destroy all the work he had accomplished.

It was beyond him, Christoph said. *He needed time to grow into music like this*, Christoph said.

Yet the notes and harmonies, the rhythms and delicacies that had been snatched from his hand had already been burned into his soul. And they would never stop driving Bach into the night hours, into the deepest reaches of his spirit, into the enthralling presence of God where he could somehow hear music from another world and translate it into notes on the staff.

Forever after—whether as an organist in the hamlets of Arnstadt or Mühlhausen, or as a chamber musician and concert master in Weimar, or as a director of music in Leipzig—when he would sit down before the blank, foreboding lines of manuscript paper, he would scratch two simple words at the top:

Jesu Juva. "Jesus, help me."

> "The aim and final reason of all music should be none else but the glory of God and the recreation of the mind. Where this is not observed, there will be no real music but only a devilish hubbub."

Then . . . from far beyond human skill, the music would begin to play. A melody would begin to form. Then somehow, another. Another melody. Different from the first. With both hands he would knit their twin songs into one—these two counterpoints—until masterfully, almost miraculously, the opposites would attract. Harmony out of diversity. Contradiction, yet unity. And where the lyrics would speak (let's say) of "a troubled heart," the violins would be told to tremble their bows. Where a soul would be described as "swimming in tears," the orchestration would undulate as if afloat. Where it would be said that the Apostle Peter "wept bitterly" after denying the Christ, or where cords and whips scourged the back of the Savior, the music would give the scenes an audible voice, a tragic pain, a driving rhythm.

It was work. Hard work. Especially for a man who considered "everything to be possible," who never thought of any musical construction as being "not feasible," who never allowed himself to settle for anything less than perfection, believing that "God, who has not known a work of imperfection, must be most pleased with the most perfect art."

And Bach's art remains even today about as close to perfect as it gets.

So when the last note had been affixed, when the convergence of consonance and dissonance had resolved into a united voice of praise, Bach would dip his pen one last time into the inkwell. To give the great work his signature? To cap off hours of wrestling and sweating by basking in his brilliance?

"The thorough bass is the most perfect foundation of music, being played with both hands in order to make a well sounding harmony to the glory of God."

No. Instead he would write the letters SDG.

Soli Deo Gloria. "To God alone be glory."

For Bach understood that all things orderly and beautiful descend from above. He could delve into his extensive library of theological books or into Luther's translation of the Bible, and find in the Word of God a form and poetry that moved him to tears—and always back to the writing desk, to put God's Word afresh to music. He could read, for example, even the laborious listings of 1 Chronicles 25 and find "this chapter to be the true foundation of all God-pleasing music."

But his eye would ever be drawn to the words of 2 Chronicles 5:13, where Solomon is seen leading all of Israel in transporting the precious ark of the covenant to the newly built temple. The priests are purified and lined up by divisions. The musicians are assembled on the east side of the altar, dressed in fine linen, playing their cymbals, harps, and lyres . . . when at the perfect time, 120 trumpets join the symphony, and a chorus of singers echo in unison, "with one voice, to praise and thank the Lord." Then the temple is filled with what appears like a cloud, and the priests assigned to preside over the service can do nothing but weep, so thick and tangible is the moment. "For the glory of the Lord filled God's temple." And all the earth could do was wait . . . and wonder . . . and worship.

And to Bach, it should always be like that. "At a reverent performance of music, God is always at hand with His gracious presence."

Always.

Seventy-five years after Bach's death, a young Felix Mendelssohn rediscovered his music—a body of work praised during Bach's lifetime but long since ignored. On March 11, 1829, he assembled orchestra and chorus for the first performance of Bach's *Passion of St. Matthew* to be heard in generations. One man in attendance exclaimed that "never have I felt a holier solemnity in a congregation than in the performers and audience that evening."

For "at a reverent performance of music, God is always at hand with His gracious presence."

Always.

This very day in Japan, a culture largely resistant to Christian influence, the music of Bach is enjoying a resurgence of popularity. In a nation where the Bible is taboo, the Japanese are now hearing the gospel in a different way—through music. From recent reports, thousands of Japanese are converting to Christianity simply by listening to the lyrics of Bach's cantatas.

How can it be that a composer and keyboardist who has been dead for 250 years is continuing to live up to his name as the "fifth evangelist" . . . and to his music as the "fifth gospel?"

Because he considered nothing impossible. Because he did everything for the glory of God. And everywhere his work continues to play, "God is always at hand with His gracious presence."

Always.

WHAT'S YOUR STORY?

Bach chose to persevere when it would have been easier to punt. He chose to let God get the glory when his own abilities caused some listeners to wonder whether it was Bach at the organ or an angel from heaven. How are you approaching the work God has given you today? As something you perform just well enough to put food on the table? Or as something you do to the glory of God—to the end of your strength?

Psalm 66:1-4 • Colossians 3:16-17 • 1 Peter 4:7-11

CLARA BARTON

There is no fear in love; instead, perfect love drives out fear, because fear involves punishment. So the one who fears has not reached perfection in love.

—1 John 4:18

CLARA BARTON

LOVE AND WAR

WASHINGTON, D.C. · 1861

Put yourself in the Civil War.

It's not the age of bomber jets picking off targets with radar precision, then roaring back unharmed to refuel and run another. It's not primarily an engagement of sneak attacks but of sheer numbers, of two opposing battle lines awaiting the sunrise, awaiting their orders, charging with chins high into the enemy's bullets, knowing that the winner will not be the side that's still standing but merely the side with the *most* still standing. Many will be mowed down even in victory.

This is not a war of annihilation but of attrition.

So even before the smoke clears, the dead litter the hillsides. The booms of cannonfire dissolve into the groans and cries of the wounded. The sights and sounds are horrifying. Blood. Bawling. Body parts.

The army doctors do their best to ease the soldier's pain, to perform miracles. But with only two hands to work with, they can't provide even basic treatment to all who need it. And even if they could, their supplies sometimes dwindle to the few bottles of chloroform in their pocket, bandages smeared with others' blood, sponges rinsed in dirty water.

Dire need is piled higher than the amputated limbs they've tossed behind the operating tents. This is vile suffering. This is pure horror.

This is gross.

But in the midst of such agony, a 40-ish woman is calmly moving from bedside to bedside, carrying a cup of hot soup or a piece of dry toast, rewetting a soldier's dressing or stopping to transcribe a letter to a wife or mother back home. Moving into the doctor's area, she ties a clean apron around a surgeon's waist, attends his request for tools and tourniquets, throws a sheet over a table and prepares a meal for the medics to have later with tea and coffee.

She's not in uniform. She's not a trained or registered nurse. She seems out of place, yet she seems to have the *run* of the place. A Union general would once be quoted as saying, "Honor any request that Miss Barton makes without question. She out-ranks me."

Clara Barton is here. This is where she works. At the front lines. In the heat of battle. Fearless amid scenes that would send most of us into shock.

"If our work is acceptable to Him who gave us the courage, protection, and strength to perform it, we need care little more."

But it wasn't always that way.

When Clara was a young teenager, her mother had sought the services of a leading doctor, trying to see if there was some medical reason for her daughter's extreme shyness. Clara was bright—brighter than most. She was a tomboy of sorts, able to handle a horse and drive a straight nail. But what Clara remembered more than anything from her childhood could be captured in one word: *Fear!*

She recalled being afraid to go to sleep at night for fear of having nightmares, seeing ghostly shapes in the clouds overhead, growing hysterical at the approach of a thunderstorm, fainting at the sight of an ox being slaughtered. (We can sort of excuse her that one.) But whether in trying to relate to other people, or be confident in her work, or think beyond a day's perceived problems, she retreated into herself, too shy even to tell her parents when her gloves had worn out or when she shivered with cold in church.

But she had a favorite verse she liked to quote to herself—a verse that had a way of lifting her head for a moment, a touch of truth that could break the icy grip of timidity and give her the courage to do and to dream.

This was it: "Perfect love casteth out fear."

"My business is stanching blood and feeding fainting men; my post the open field between the bullet and the hospital. I make gruel, not speeches. I write letters home for wounded soldiers, not political addresses."

The doctor apparently picked up on this sliver of light in her otherwise depressing world, for when his examination turned up nothing conclusive, he gave Clara's mother this insightful piece of advice: "She will never assert herself for her own sake. She will suffer wrong first. But for others she will be perfectly fearless." So he advised Mrs. Barton to "throw responsibility on her. She has all the qualities of a teacher. As soon as her age will permit, give her a school to teach."

The age her mother would permit turned out to be fifteen. And Clara continued to teach for nearly 20 years, even originating the first public school in New Jersey—only to be passed over when the rolls had swelled to 600 students and the decision-makers concluded that a frail woman had no business being headmaster.

Anger and disillusionment drove her in a new direction—to the nation's capital. But heads rolled in her department at the U.S. Patent Office when the presidency changed hands in 1856, and she would have to wait four more years before returning to Washington under the Lincoln administration.

But (we all know now) tough years were to follow. Civil War erupted in 1861. And when Clara learned that a regiment from her home state of Massachusetts had been attacked and stripped of its baggage in Baltimore and was being shipped in to Washington for surgery and treatment, she rushed down to the temporary hospital being set up at the train station. Seeing the supplies running low, she ran home to tear up old sheets and towels, returning with a full basket of cloths and bandages.

The sight of blood, the screams of soldiers enduring surgeries without anesthesia clutched at her heart. But where fear couldn't go, love could. And love—love of God, love of country, love for her old pupils who lay dying in Union blue—drove her beyond fear. Beyond herself.

The next day she ventured into the streets seeking supplies and help. Then she petitioned the *Worcester Daily* newspaper back home to spread the word that their sons and husbands were dying for lack of medical equipment, necessities, clean socks, proper food.

"We trust we are ready to bind the wounds or bear those of our own, if necessary. I shall remain here while anyone remains, and do whatever comes to my hand. I may be compelled to face danger but never to fear it, and while our soldiers can stand and fight, I can stand and feed and nurse them."

She would be true to those words throughout the war, even when a bullet pierced the sleeve of her dress as she held a cup of water to a dying man's lips, even when she had to use her own pocketknife to dig shards of shrapnel from a man's face in the field, even when she had to go without sleep or food for days on end.

But how? "God gives you the strength, and the thing that seemed impossible is done."

After the war, she worked to reunite missing soldiers with their families. But when illness drove her overseas to seek rest, she found herself back on the battlefield amidst the Franco-Prussian War, where she learned of the work of the Red Cross and vowed to bring back its lifesaving mission with her to the States. Through years of persistent lobbying, this 5-foot female whose life had begun in slavery to fear would found the American Red Cross and run its operation hands-on into the twentieth century.

Still active at over 80 years old, in one of her final acts as president, she led the Red Cross efforts during a typhoid outbreak in Butler, Pennsylvania. It was bad. Up to 40 people were dying every day. But a man who watched her working to aid the suffering "pictured the light of her lantern going on and on through the night until it stopped over the stricken town of Butler, and the people there looked upon it as the light of a great soul that had come to them out of the darkness, bringing comfort and healing and the calm spirit that banishes all fear."

Look closer into the light, and you'd have seen the face of love.

WHAT'S YOUR STORY?

What does fear stop you from doing? Putting a legitimate gift in the offering plate instead of tipping God a few dollars? Shaking hands with a homeless man who hasn't had a caring touch in years? Giving your whole life to Christ—lock, stock, and barrel—without holding on to a handful of petty quirks and unseemly entertainment habits? When you lose yourself in love to God, one of the first things to go is fear. For when He comes first, your own worries won't last.

Joshua 1:6-9 • Isaiah 35:3-10 • Romans 8:12-17

DIETRICH
BONHOEFFER

"As for you, are you seeking great things for yourself? Stop that, for look, I am bringing disaster on everyone," says the Lord, "but I have given to you your life as a reward wherever you go."

—Jeremiah 45:5

DIETRICH
BONHOEFFER
THE HUNTED

BERLIN, GERMANY · 1943

By almost everyone's accounts, Dietrich Bonhoeffer was a great man. Questionable in his theology, maybe, but passionately articulate. Ramrod straight. From the click of his heels to the steely gaze of his eyes, his whole demeanor was spit-polish perfection. But his inevitable rise to prominence would be restrained by an even more powerful rise of conscience. His greatness would not be found in achieving the fame of men but in defying the defamers of God.

For God had shown him what to expect from life—not to seek "great things for yourself . . . for look, I am bringing disaster on all flesh, says the Lord, but I have given to you your life as a reward wherever you go." He would write from his Tegel prison cell: "I cannot get away from Jeremiah 45."

But for the first few years of his theological career, *he* was the one doing the hunting—screaming to wake up a sleeping church that was nodding in lockstep with the Nazis' appeal to patriotism, youthful discipline, law and order. The humiliation of World War I had left the Germans weary, weakened, and without heroes, making this rising tide of German pride a welcome new throb in the national heartbeat. The church perceived "the saving of our nation by our leader Adolf Hitler as a gift from God's hand."

Even from this many years out, a statement like that has the ability to chill. But for the faithful who were living it before their very eyes, ice melted into fury.

And Bonhoeffer was among the most ferocious.

When hard-line leaders in the church began denying ordination to anyone of non-Aryan descent, Bonhoeffer called for all ministers to resign in solidarity. When they declared the Jews a "separate, inferior race," he helped rally what remained of the faithful remnant into a Confessing Church movement that refused to exclude anyone from the gospel. And when Jewish businesses began being boycotted and boarded up, he sounded the alarm for the church "not only to help the victims who have fallen under the wheel, but [if necessary] to fall into the spokes of the wheel itself."

He had accepted the challenge. And he expected to win.

Only once did he blink. He had many influential friends and colleagues in church circles around the world. He had studied with distinction for a year in New York. He had pastored for two years at a German-speaking church in London after turning down a similar position in Berlin out of protest. He had spoken at international Christian gatherings, warning both the foreign preachers and the press that his homeland was in trouble—that the Nazis were depriving Jews of citizenship, repealing basic human rights and freedoms, and hurtling pell-mell toward dictatorship with a madman at the helm.

"God is just, whether or not we understand His ways. God is just, whether He corrects and chastises us or pardons us. We don't see it, but our faith must acknowledge: God alone is just."

By this time the German church had already demanded that he cut ties with his contacts overseas. The German Foreign Office had told him to keep his mouth shut if he knew what was good for him. And a high-level government decree had slammed the door on his little seminary, forcing him to travel in secret from town to town in order to supervise Confessing Church pastors serving illegally in small parishes. Church offerings were being seized. Informers were running to the authorities with sermon notes and pulpit announcements. Hitler's minister of church affairs had declared that "belief in the Son of God" was a "laughable dogma of the past."

Now Bonhoeffer had become one of the hunted.

So in June 1939, despondent over his country's condition, he conceded to take his foreign friends up on their offer—a safe teaching position at Union Seminary in New York City. For he knew war was just a matter of time, he knew he could never fight in the German army, and he knew he would be killed for standing his ground.

"God's Word doesn't promise us that we will be victorious over sin and death. Rather, it says with all its might that someone has won this victory, and that this person, if we have him as Lord, will also win the victory over us."

But almost immediately upon his arrival in the States, he realized his heart was an ocean away. "I have made a mistake in coming to America. I shall have no right to take part in the restoration of Christian life in Germany after the war unless I share the trials of this time with my people. . . .

Christians in Germany will face the terrible alternative of either willing the defeat of their nation in order that Christian civilization may survive, or willing the victory of their nation and thereby destroying our civilization. I know which of these alternatives I must choose; but I cannot make this choice in security."

After a month of unsettled freedom, he resettled in Germany as a fugitive.

Within a few years, he was corralled into custody for acts of treason. Those among the Nazi elite who were secretly plotting a political overthrow of Hitler's regime had tapped Bonhoeffer to work in—(wink, wink)—"counter-intelligence." But in reality, rather than keeping his ear close to the ground in foreign soil, he had been feeding incriminating information to his foreign sources, trying to help put together a multi-national effort against the Nazis, and spiriting Jews out of Germany into Switzerland.

But through paranoia and paper trails, the underground resistance was eventually brought into the light. Bonhoeffer—who once represented the greatness of Germany—was going to jail as a German traitor.

One year passed in isolation. In his second year he was transferred to the dreaded Gestapo prison. But by Easter Sunday 1945, he and the other select prisoners who had been loaded onto trucks and shipped to a more secure location could hear American guns booming in the distance. The Allies were advancing, the Germans were in retreat, the war couldn't last much longer.

Could freedom be just around the corner? You might say that.

But Bonhoeffer had once said it much better: "Long did we seek you—freedom—in discipline, action, and suffering. Now that we die, in the face of God Himself, we behold you."

So while hoping for release and a return to his love of study and preaching, he braced himself for the ultimate sacrifice.

"One must completely abandon any attempt to make something of oneself. . . . In so doing we throw ourselves completely into the arms of God, taking seriously, not our own sufferings, but those of God in the world—watching with Christ in Gethsemane. . . . That is how one becomes a man (see Jeremiah 45!). How can success make us arrogant, or failure lead us astray, when we share in God's sufferings through a life of this kind?"

The following Sunday, he and a few others who had been herded into a van and driven into the German countryside, stopped at a schoolhouse where Bonhoeffer was allowed to lead his fellow prisoners in a worship service. The final "amen" was followed by words that for a weaker man would have sounded more final: "Prisoner Bonhoeffer, come with us."

A doctor on duty that morning finishes the story: "Through the half-open door in one room of the huts, I saw Pastor Bonhoeffer, before taking off his prison garb, kneeling on the floor praying fervently to his God. I was most deeply moved by the way this lovable man prayed, so devout and so certain that God heard his prayer. At the place of execution, he again said a short prayer and then climbed the steps to the gallows, brave and composed. His death ensued after a few seconds. In the almost fifty years I have worked as a doctor, I have hardly ever seen a man die so entirely submissive to the will of God."

That's greatness for you.

WHAT'S YOUR STORY?

Some things are worth fighting for. Even though most of us are content with living peaceful lives, trying not to make unnecessary waves, and tolerating other people's rights to have an opinion, there are times and reasons for running the risk of a judgmental reputation and taking a stand for what you know is right. Have you come up against one of those lately? Are you willing to be a light in the darkness?

Jeremiah 6:10-19 • Luke 12:1-12 • Ephesians 5:6-13

WILLIAM BOOTH

"I was hungry and you gave Me something to eat; I was thirsty and you gave Me something to drink; I was a stranger and you took Me in."

—Matthew 25:35

WILLIAM
BOOTH
I WAS HUNGRY

LONDON, ENGLAND · 1890

One of 1890's hottest best-sellers was a book by journalist and explorer Henry Morgan Stanley—the same Stanley who had been dispatched by the *New York Herald* in 1870 to locate geographer David Livingstone's whereabouts on the Dark Continent—("Mr. Livingstone, I presume?") *In Darkest Africa* was the real-life, adventurous account of Stanley's later expedition to rescue a native governor from a Moslem uprising, and was as rich with lush, jungle imagery as it was with drama and intrigue. The dense, towering trees. The thick, muggy air. Shrieks and growls from the thicket. Life-and-death at every turn.

William Booth couldn't put it down.

But as the candlelight flickered against the pages, he began to see a connection between the oppressive African bush and a world he knew much better. And firsthand: the slums of London's East Side—and the many others throughout the country where thousands upon thousands knew only the darkness of dire poverty, the raucous noise of the ale-house, the stench of raw sewage.

Sure, Africa had its slave traders and ivory hunters. But didn't England have its own traders in human lives—men who profited from the careless choices of the weak and desperate? Yes, the jungle pygmies knew only the small realm of their own tribal territory, never dreaming that a bigger world might exist beyond. But did Britain's drunks, bums, and brothel workers have any better hope of ever rising above the squalor, of ever escaping to a life of peace, order, and respectability?

At least one man thought so. And playing off the popularity of Stanley's title, Booth pulled his ideas into a book of his own and called it . . . *In Darkest England and the Way Out.*

It was an appeal to restore hope to the poor—through labor offices that could help the unemployed find work, through farms equipped for job retraining, through banks that provided short-term loans so that craftsmen could buy back their own tools from the pawn shops. He called for cheap meals, lodging for the homeless, basic necessities for needy families.

But not everyone liked what they read. They accused him of tampering with the trade unions, of advocating socialism, of using the guise of popular reforms to mask his religious intentions.

Oh yeah? Who's masking it? "Surely it is better for these miserable, wretched crowds to have food to eat, clothes to wear, and a home in which to lay their weary bones than for them to be hungry, and naked, and homeless, and possess no religion at all."

For Booth understood that a full stomach with an empty soul was worthless. He knew that prosperity on earth with no treasure in heaven was the most deceitful form of destitution. But when both of these needs were met together, the result was complete relief. "While we desire to feed the hungry, and clothe the naked, and

"However poor you may be, however wretched you may be, however bad you may be, you have two friends. One is Jesus Christ, and the other is the Salvation Army!"

provide shelter for the shelterless, we are still more anxious to bring about that regeneration of heart and life which is essential to their future happiness."

"If these people are to believe in Jesus Christ, become the servants of God, and escape the miseries of the wrath to come, they must be helped out of their present miseries."

He should know. He had been doing it for nearly 40 years—ever since that hot, July night in 1865 when he had walked home through the grimy streets of East London, seeing five-year-olds staggering blind drunk in the bar-room doorways, children making toys out of chicken bones, mothers forcing beer down their babies' throats, men lost in liquor and fist-fighting in the alley. For 13 years he had been trying to pastor, trying to discover what he could do to let God "have all there was of William Booth." But somehow here, in the hollow eyes of the outcast, he discovered a new calling. A new congregation.

A new credo from Christ Himself: "I was hungry and you gave Me something to eat; I was thirsty and you gave Me something to drink; I was a stranger and you took Me in. . . . Whatever you did for one of the least of these brothers, you did for Me."

The whole way home that night, he grappled with his feelings. Why was he grieving like this for the derelicts? Why hurting so for the homeless? And why stewing with equal passion against churches where the private pews of the rich sat empty for months at a time while the poor who had the guts to attend were treated as second-class scum, and the millions more who never felt worthy to darken a church door for fear of like treatment were left to fend for themselves—and find God's help for their own souls (if they had one).

It was nearly midnight when Booth's wife, Catherine, heard his key turning in the lock, his six children already asleep but his mind wide awake.

"Darling," he said, before speaking another word, "I have found my destiny."

And it wouldn't be easy on any of them.

They soon began setting up evangelistic meetings, seeking the poor and unprofitable as their audience. Shut out of the churches and chapels, they rented parks or public buildings, erecting tents a stone's throw from the slums, drawing curious crowds to the fire of their oil-burning lamps. "Come drunk or sober!" went out the invitation.

And it grew. By 1878 they and their growing "Salvation Army" had set up more than two dozen stations for preaching the gospel. They had created lunchrooms where the poor could buy hot soup or even a three-course meal for pennies. They had gotten in the habit of distributing Christmas dinners through the streets of London, and setting the course for what would become a worldwide ministry that today feeds the hungry and serves the sick in more than 100 nations.

Why? Very simple. "We saw the need, we saw the people starving, we saw people going about half-naked, people doing sweated labor, and we set about bringing a remedy for these things.

"We were obliged. There was a compulsion. How could you do anything else?"

Booth never stopped working *In Darkest England*—and in the darkest places of the U.S. and the world—showing the defeated, displaced, and downtrodden the *Way Out* through the Word of God.

In one of his final sermons, in January of 1912, before a crowd of 7,000 at London's Albert Hall, he rallied his Army in typical fighting form: "While women weep as they do now, I'll fight. While little children go hungry as they do now, I'll fight. While men go to prison—in and out, in and out—I'll fight. While there yet remains one dark soul without the light of God, I'll fight.

"I'll fight to the very end!"

The end came that August. Forty thousand people filled the auditorium to pay their respects. Even Queen Mary, a staunch admirer of Booth and his work, chose at the last minute to attend. No place had been made for her, so she took her place among the common folk—right next to a one-time prostitute who had been told by General Booth shortly before his death that one day, "when you get to heaven, you'll have a place of honor."

On his casket rested a small knot of three faded, red carnations—the only flowers that lay there—placed by this young girl who had gotten close enough to set them unobtrusively on the glass lid.

She wiped away her tears as the service came to a close, shyly catching the eye of the queen, and saying to her through gentle sobs, "He cared for the likes of us."

Yes. Because he saw Jesus in them.

WHAT'S YOUR STORY?

Trying to do something for the poor, the homeless, the widowed, the sick—it's hard work, no two ways about it. You run the risk of being burned, taken advantage of, used and used up. But how can we deny that a warm blanket for a cold night, a sack of groceries for a shut-in, or a hamburger and fries for the man holding up a "Help" sign at the corner are not acts closer than most to the heart of God?

Deuteronomy 15:7-11 • Isaiah 58:6-12 • Luke 14:12-14

DAVID
BRAINERD

Jesus stood up and cried out, "If anyone
is thirsty, he should come to Me and
drink!"

—John 7:37

DAVID
BRAINERD
A THIRST FOR GOD

CROSSWEEKSUNG, NEW JERSEY · 1745

Sick.

And tired.

So what else was new?

It was about the only life David Brainerd had ever known. Even as a boy he had been weak, congested, feverish. Twice he had started the fall term at Yale College only to be sent home early—once with the measles, once spitting up blood and showing all the telltale signs of the tuberculosis that would eventually take his life.

But was it really tuberculosis that shortened his years on earth to less than thirty? Could he perhaps have lived much longer—even *with* that consuming illness—had he stayed in the city, close to decent medical care, warm and dry under his own roof?

There was a day, perhaps, when he would have settled for such a tranquil life—pastoring a quiet church in Long Island, losing himself in his studies and writings, marrying the girl who had captured his affections and even helped care for him through his final days.

But something just didn't taste right about it.

"I've resolved that in my future ministry, I will not enter into other men's labors," David wrote in his now-famous journals, "neither will I settle down where the gospel was preached before. Ease and comfort shall never determine me!" Only thirst.

Thirst for God. Thirst for obedience. And by the late fall of 1743, kicked out of Yale for privately questioning a professor's spirituality, licensed to preach but with no pulpit to call his own, a new kind of thirst: a growing desire for the salvation of the Indians.

It happened slowly. First came the call from a Scottish missionary society for someone to take the gospel to the Pennsylvania Indians living at the Forks of the Delaware River. One of the group's commissioners in New Jersey who had taken a liking to David and who knew of his uncertain situation thought he'd be perfect for the job. David wasn't so sure. Yet he agreed to try.

"It is impossible for any rational creature to be happy without acting all for God. God Himself could not make him happy any other way."

The taste test wasn't long in coming.

One bitterly cold day a few weeks later, he set out on horseback for a missionary meeting in New York, when somewhere along the 50-mile trek to the Long Island ferry, a vicious blizzard slammed hard into his path. Bracing himself against the stinging elements, coughing clouds of white steam through his shivering fists, his future began to flash before his eyes. "This will be my life in the Delaware wilderness. Can I endure it? Should I not turn back? O God, it would be far less difficult to lie down in the grave."

But suddenly, forming words with his mouth that opposed everything else his barking lungs and human nature were saying, he cried out into the blinding whiteness, "O God, I choose to go rather than to stay!"

He had found his fountain.

As he would say later, "I want to wear my life out in His service and for His glory."

So in March of the next year, he hacked his way alone into the wild, screeching forests of the untamed American Northeast. His original destination being declared too dangerous by the missionary board, he settled down instead in a wigwam a mile or so distant from the Mohegan Indians in western Massachusetts. He slept on straw. He barely ate. He braved their camps in the daylight and battled his fears through the night. He struggled to learn their language, fought wearily against his life-long scourge of depression . . .

And he prayed. Prayed till his knees would tremble. Prayed till his fingers would no longer flex. Prayed till exhaustion claimed him in sleep, and prayed at the slightest waking in the night.

"Dear Lord, my heart is ready to sink with the thoughts of my work, alone in the wilderness. But it comforts me to think of Abraham going on not knowing whither. I beseech thee, Lord, go with me."

For a solid year he worked there, starting a little school, employing an interpreter, looking for the slightest crack for the gospel to get through. But with little to show for his wearisome work, he was dispatched back to the Forks of the Delaware, where he started again from square one, fighting wicked fevers, preaching in the Indian settlements, riding for miles through the driving rain to reach neighboring tribes, sleeping uncovered in the cold and damp.

Yet somehow he found his thirst quenched "with little appearance of success to comfort me."

It had now been nearly two and a half years since he had first struck out on mission. Twenty-four months without a single convert, except for his Indian interpreter who had slowly come to faith in Christ.

David was sick. Literally sick. And tired.

And then, it happened.

August 5, 1745. "I preached . . . from John 7:37: 'Jesus stood and cried, "If any man thirst, let him come unto me, and drink." ' One or two of [the Indians] were struck with deep concern who had been little affected before; others had their concern increased to a considerable degree . . . inquiring, 'What then should we do to be saved?' And all their conversation among themselves turned upon religious matters.

"There was one woman, who had been much concerned for her soul. . . . She seemed to be filled with love for Christ . . . and appeared afraid of nothing so much as of grieving and offending Him whom her soul loved."

Christ had come to the campfire to satisfy a thirst that catches in the throat of every race, tribe, and tongue, to people who for centuries had danced before the devils—a thirst that can start in the quivering heart of a thin-faced TB sufferer like David Brainerd or in the questioning mind of an Indian woman steeped in spirit-worship and superstition . . . and find its satisfaction in the same forgiving stream.

Anyone can thirst. But only God can satisfy.

Within a matter of days the trickle became a flood. God poured out His grace, and Indians by the dozens lapped it up by the handful. Many times David returned to his favorite text, preaching about man's thirsty soul and God's refreshing supply. Within a year he was leading a church of 130 Indian believers.

But within two, he was dead from the strain—nearly 15,000 miles on horseback over the course of his three-year ministry. In his final moments, dying at the home of Jonathan Edwards on October 9, 1747, at the age of

29, the famed Puritan preacher turned to his daughter and said, "Look, he is smiling! He has been welcomed by the glorious assembly into the upper world"—where no one is sick, where no one is tired, where no one thirsts, and where all who seek His fountain are satisfied forevermore.

WHAT'S YOUR STORY?

Surely you've wished that the sweet sound of compliments, the comfort of a padded savings account, or the popcorn smell of your favorite movies would be enough to keep you content and satisfied for life. But pride and pleasure always promise more than they can deliver. Have you peeked long enough into their empty barrels to realize they can never do for you what Christ can?

Psalm 73:1-28 • John 12:20-27 • Philippians 3:7-11

JOHN
BUNYAN

You have come to Mount Zion, to the city of the living God . . . to God who is the judge of all, to the spirits of righteous people made perfect, to Jesus (mediator of a new covenant) and to the sprinkled blood.

—Hebrews 12:22-24

JOHN
BUNYAN
COME AND GET ME

BEDFORDSHIRE, ENGLAND · 1660

The rumors were true. Everyone knew it. There were going to be some special guests at this Sunday's service. Guests with badges. And weapons. And a warrant for the pastor's arrest.

So you can't say John Bunyan didn't have ample warning to save his skin. He could flee. He could hide. Shucks, if he didn't want to run the risk of being a fugitive, all he had to do was say he wouldn't gather his little church together any more, okay? That's all the Law wanted. With the Royalists back in power after the death of Oliver Cromwell, with the brief window of religious freedom that had been enjoyed after the English Civil War pressed back into place, it was technically true that anyone not sanctioned by the state church no longer had the right to preach. But this decree was more political than personal. *Tack a simple "Closed" sign on the church door, and nobody gets hurt.*

But Bunyan, stopping just short of the meeting house that Sunday, knowing that the constable would be waiting to escort him past the silent rows of worshipers, stared his options in the face—and saw only the faces of his tiny flock. "For what will my weak and newly converted brethren think of it, but that I was not so strong in deed as I was in word? If I should run, I might make them afraid to stand."

He knew this dark night of oppression and persecution might just be beginning—for him, for them, for all of England. And he knew that neither his own congregation nor his own conscience could abide a coward's way out.

"I will not stop speaking the Word of God."

Even if it means jail time?

"I shall not force or compel any man to hear me. But if I come to any place where people are met together, I will, according to the best of my skill and wisdom, exhort and counsel them to seek after the Lord Jesus Christ, for the salvation of their souls."

Even if it means you'll rot in your cell before you get out?

"He who stops preaching the Word of God for fear of the excommunication of men is already excommunicated of God, and shall in the day of judgment be counted a traitor to Christ."

Even if it means you'll swing by the neck till dead?

"If I was out of prison today, I would preach the gospel again tomorrow."

Hard to reason with a man like that.

For John Bunyan had not taken an easy path to Christ. Like C. S. Lewis in a later century, he had not come to Christ walking on air but rather kicking and screaming, figuring it was "as good to be damned for many sins as for few." Even after his conversion, he endured long, torturous temptations to recant and renounce his beliefs. But one evening, while sitting in

"I can truly say that when I have been to preach, I have gone full of guilt and terror even to the pulpit door . . . yet God carried me on, but surely with a strong hand, for neither guilt nor hell could take me off my work."

front of the fire at home with his wife, the Spirit had painted these pictures from Hebrews 12:22-24 in his mind:

"Come to Mount Zion . . . Come to the city of the living God . . . Come to God who is the judge of all . . . Come to Jesus, the mediator of a new covenant . . . Come to the sprinkled blood."

Suddenly he knew he could no longer straddle both sides of the Christian fence. His days of dabbling in doubt and denial were over.

"I must go to Jesus.

"Christ was precious to my soul that night," he wrote. "I could scarce lie in bed for joy, and peace, and triumph. Through this blessed sentence, the Lord led me over and over, first to this word, and then to that, and showed me wonderful glory in every one of them. At this my former darkness and atheism fled away, and the blessed things of heaven were set within my view."

So the black robes behind the judge's bench could pound their fists all they wanted. John Bunyan wasn't budging. He was going to Jesus—no matter how bullheaded and ignorant they thought he was.

"Of all tears, they are the best that are made by the blood of Christ; and of all joy, that is the sweetest that is mixed with mourning over Christ. Oh, it is a goodly thing to be on our knees, with Christ in our arms, before God."

Therefore he was also going to jail. First for six years. Then in and out of confinement for six years more. Twelve years of undeserved detention—twelve years of worrying how his family would survive without his income—

twelve years of leaden days and even longer nights.

But had he remained free to preach, perhaps his powerfully creative words would never have been written down, evaporating into the 17th-century English sky. For it was only in the dank, dragging hours of a pointless prison term that the Word of God truly came alive in his heart. "Those Scriptures that I saw nothing in before are made in this place and state to shine on me." With his world shrinking around him, God opened to John Bunyan the windows on another world—"Mount Zion . . . the city of the living God . . . the heavenly Jerusalem . . . myriads of angels in festive gathering . . . the assembly of the firstborn whose names have been written in heaven."

"I have seen here what I am persuaded I shall never, while in this world, be able to express."

Yet the almighty power of God, working through this old pot-and-pan mender with nothing now but time on his hands, brought that world a little closer to earth—to us—through the books and stories that flowed from the pen of a prisoner preacher who never stopped "going to Jesus." Over sixty books in all. And the best known among them is still considered one of the dozen greatest books in the English language.

The Pilgrim's Progress.

Throughout the early American pioneer days, families who owned any books at all usually possessed only two: a Holy Bible and a copy of Bunyan's celebrated classic—to inspire them to godly living.

Today it has been translated into more than 200 languages and continues to draw people to Christ 300-plus years after its first publication.

John Bunyan had seen his persecution in perspective. "Let the rage and malice of men be never so great, they can do no more, nor go any farther than God permits them. But when they have done their worst, 'We know that all things work together for good to those that love God.' "

To those who never stop "going to Jesus."

WHAT'S YOUR STORY?

The shortest distance between you and a meaningful life is a straight line to Jesus Christ. It's not the safest route. It won't necessarily get you a better job, put your name on an invitation list, or move the decimal place up on your spending money. But as these passages say, when nothing else matters to you but pleasing God, no one can steal your joy.

Daniel 3:8-18 • 1 Timothy 6:11-16 • 1 Peter 3:13-16

JOHN
CALVIN

"Blessed are you when they insult you and persecute you, and say every kind of evil against you falsely, because of Me. Be glad and rejoice, because your reward is great in heaven. For that is how they persecuted the prophets who were before you."

—Matthew 5:11-12

JOHN CALVIN
THE HIGH ROAD

BASEL, SWITZERLAND · 1535

John Calvin's conscience was never built for the main road.

Yet the prevailing religion of his day never thought of straying from it, being grossly overparked at the intersection of political power and sheer manipulation. And as far as Calvin was concerned, it was high time somebody had the courage to check the meter.

So when his doctor friend Nicholas Cop had the opportunity to speak before the assembled faculty and students at the University in Paris in 1533, Calvin urged him, "Give the pure Word a chance in your address. After centuries of silence, let truth be proclaimed from the pulpit."

Some historians say Calvin's hand was the one that actually wrote Cop's script. But whoever was responsible, they were both button-holed with the blame.

Strange how words like these could cause such an uproar: " 'Blessed shall you be,' Jesus said, 'when for my sake men shall despise you and persecute you and say evil against you falsely.' The world is accustomed to call those who strive to spread the pure gospel—and who believe that by doing so they are obeying God—heretics, seducers, imposters, and slanderers. But blessed and worthy of envy are those who bear all this with serenity. 'Rejoice,' He says, 'for your reward is great in heaven.'

"Come then, Christian men, let us strain our every nerve for this blessedness. God, who by His Word brings to birth faith, hope, and charity, draws us by His grace. He opens our minds so that we may believe the gospel, so that we may understand that there is only one God who alone must be served with all our soul and in whose name we must bear all and suffer all."

But somehow such a call to Christian courage and evangelism hit the wrong ears as inflammatory, and the French Parliament moved swiftly to drag the two men in by their shirttails.

Both, however, had found the back door unlocked in Paris and had gotten out before they could be taken for questioning.

"We cannot be Christ's soldiers on any other condition than to have the greater part of the world rising in hostility against us."

But the king wanted everyone else to know this much: "We are very distressed and displeased that in our fair city of Paris, head and principal city of our kingdom, where stands the principal university of the whole of Christendom—[*the main road if ever there was one*]—this accursed, heretical sect should be breeding where many others might follow its example. With all our power and might we wish to prevent this, without sparing anyone. For this reason we wish and intend that such a grievous punishment shall be given them that it shall be both a correction to the accursed heretics and an example for all the others!"

So every township in France now had royal license to not only *sniff* out but also *snuff* out anyone holding views in opposition to the official church line. And to have fun doing it.

It was my way or the highway. Stay on the main road or become a greasy spot right in the middle of it.

For a year Calvin skittered from one town to another, learning the French backroads like the back of his hand before slipping out of the country entirely in late 1534, showing up practically penniless in Basel, Switzerland.

But back in France, the heat had only gotten hotter for his countrymen. Some had continued to protest both the king's decree and the church's degenerating doctrine. Hundreds had been arrested. More than 20 had been executed. One of them, in fact, was a personal friend of Calvin's.

The king, eager to maintain alliances with the surrounding nations, misrepresented the character of his captives, warning the Swiss and Germans to protect their own countries as well by taking sweeping action against these enemies of peace and civil order who sought refuge within their borders.

> "He who strays away from the Word of God may run as fast as he likes, yet he will not reach the goal because he will wind up in the wrong path. Better to limp on the right way than to run in the wrong."

So Calvin was no safer in Switzerland than at the palace in Paris. Wouldn't it be better at this point just to climb back on the main road? Wasn't that his only road to survival?

No. For Calvin there was only one road—the road of obedience, the path of truth, the one that rarely met with people's approval but shined like the sun with the glory of God.

"For my part, seeing that these false plotters were trying to effect not only the burial of this shedding of blood by heaping unfounded charges upon the holy martyrs after their death, but also seeking the means to proceed to the last extremity of killing the poor faithful without anyone being able to take pity on them, it seemed to me that unless I was strongly opposed to this—as far as in me lay—I could not exonerate myself from the charge of disloyalty if I remained silent.

"And this was the reason which spurred me on to publish my *Institutes of the Christian Religion*, in order to reply to these evil charges which others were sowing, and to clear my brothers, whose death was precious before the Lord. . . . It had no other object but that people should be informed of the faith that was held by those whom evil and lawless flatterers were vilifying in a foul and most mischievous way."

Ah, the *Institutes*. That massive multi-volume set—the same one that is still in print, still sitting on the bookshelves of the serious scholar—was at first only a booklet, not merely coughed into the air as a collection of dusty doctrines but launched into the high humidity of real-world events . . . to defend his fallen heroes with a pen that was truly mightier than the sword.

Calvin boldly explained that they had not died in vain.

Yet his were not words forged in human bravery and courage. By his own admission Calvin was an inwardly retiring and timid man. If he could have had things his way, he would have gladly spent the rest of his life in quiet study and ponderous reflection. "But I have learned from experience that we cannot see very far before us. When I promised myself an easy, tranquil life, what I least expected was at hand."

After a brief return to France, he found himself detoured by war into Geneva, Switzerland, where he spent most of his remaining years leading Protestant reforms that literally reshaped church history.

Of course, not everyone took to his reforming ways. More than once his enemies threatened to throw him headfirst into the river. Mobs sometimes formed at night outside his door, saluting him in derision with the repeated flare of gunshots.

But constrained by that conscience of his, he would preach God's truth day and night from the pulpit, defending its precious words on pain of death, even flinging his arms around the Communion vessels when the unsaved insisted on their freedom to partake, crying, "These hands you may crush, these arms you may lop off, my life you may take. My blood is yours; you may have it. But you shall never force me to give holy things to the profaned and dishonor the table of my God!"

God would bless the reviled and persecuted.

And God's blessing was all that mattered.

"Should we exchange a comfortable life for one of continual wandering, and our full grain bins for the bread of misery in foreign lands? Yes. And if you think that such a life is preposterous, you are no longer a true Christian. It is hard—how well I know it—to leave one's home in order to become a pilgrim. And yet the Lord transforms this destiny, which in the eyes of men is so harsh, into sheer joy."

The joy of the high road.

WHAT'S YOUR STORY?

If you were expecting the Christian life to be a pleasure trip, someone was guilty of false advertising. Being faithful to God and His Word will always come at a price. Sure, some will applaud your godly virtue, but you'll have plenty of others to malign your character and question your motives. The reward of the righteous rarely comes from the crowd but always from Christ. And that's reward enough.

Isaiah 66:5-6 • John 15:18-25 • 2 Timothy 3:10-17

WILLIAM
CAREY

Therefore, brothers, by the mercies of God, I urge you to present your bodies as a living sacrifice, holy and pleasing to God; this is your spiritual worship.

—Romans 12:1

WILLIAM
CAREY
LIVING SACRIFICE

CALCUTTA, INDIA · 1794

William Carey was a man of many verses.

Even as a young cobbler's apprentice, he was captivated one day by a sermon based on Hebrews 13:13—an appeal to go to Christ "outside the camp, bearing His disgrace." For the first time in his new Christian life, he understood that raw form and ritual would never be enough to satisfy the soul's hunger for God. True faith meant going outside the lines, outside the box, outside the "camp" of stuffy, stifling religion—where others see disgrace, but where believers sense His pleasure.

He is also known for one of Christian history's most inspiring sermons—a message based on Isaiah 54:2-3 that called the church to "enlarge" its tent and "stretch out" its hand to the lost and dying in other nations. He ended with words that still echo today across the fields and frontiers of foreign missions: "Expect great things *from* God. Attempt great things *for* God."

These are the kinds of challenges and convictions that get people like William Carey branded by even their fellow churchmen as "miserable enthusiasts" and men "gone mad." At a meeting of ministers where Carey simply lobbed the idea for a missionary program onto the discussion table, one of the leading members thundered back, "Young man, sit down! When God pleases to convert the heathen, He will do it without your aid or mine!"

But they're also the kinds of challenges and convictions that give people like William Carey a need for *another* verse—a message God can use not only to help them defend their actions but also soothe their depression, a Word that not only compels but comforts.

William Carey had that kind of a verse.

It first showed up in a letter to his father shortly after becoming convinced that God was calling him to pull up stakes and leave for India. Admittedly, what he was attempting to do seemed crazy. Looking at it from any viewpoint other than God's would have left you scratching your head to understand or—if you cared about William at all—eager to do *anything* to help him change his mind.

"O what I would give for a kind and sympathetic friend such as I had in England. But I rejoice that I am here, notwithstanding; and God is here, who not only can have compassion, but is able to save to the uttermost."

Even his wife refused to go along. Not only was she still mourning the recent death of their two-year-old daughter, she also had three boys at home to raise—and was a scant three weeks away from delivering another! The last thing she needed at the moment was a five-month boat ride through wartime waters. What husband shouldn't understand *that?*

So, yes, the sensitive, modern male has trouble explaining the timing of Carey's venture. He himself had his doubts. Yet he gave his father the only explanation he had for going: "The importance of spending our time for God alone is the principal theme of the gospel. 'I beseech you, brethren,' says Paul, 'by the mercies of God, that you present your bodies a living sacrifice, holy and acceptable, which is your reasonable service.' To be devoted like a sacrifice to holy uses is the great business of a Christian.

"I hope, dear father, you may be enabled to surrender me up to the Lord for the most arduous, honorable, and important work that ever any of the sons of men were called to engage in. I have many sacrifices to make. I must part with a beloved family and a number of most affectionate friends. But I have set my hand to the plow."

As it turned out, war declarations between France and Great Britain prevented his vessel from leaving on schedule. And by the time he had secured passage on another ship six weeks later, he had persuaded his wife (now with a three-week-old newborn in tow) to journey along with him.

Their voyage was long and monotonous. Patience wore thin. Spiritual disciplines wore thinner. Carey confessed to having "no more of the spiritual warfare maintained in my soul, and no more communion with God. . . . I have need to read the Word of God more, and above all, I want a heart to feed on it." As often as he could, he clung to Deuteronomy 33:25—the promise that God would give him strength equal to his days. And when an angry storm flashed its teeth as they rounded the southern tip of Africa, launching waves that appeared (to Carey's eyes) to tower 50, 60 yards above them, for a while it didn't look like he had too many days left.

"You have been speaking about Dr. Carey, Dr. Carey. When I am gone, say nothing about Dr. Carey. Speak about Dr. Carey's Savior."

The journey to India finally over, they settled into even more trouble. Carey's only friend in India—his sponsor and guide, John Thomas—had not been totally aboveboard about his personal problems with money. Before long, the man had used most of Carey's meager savings to pay off his own debts and resume his lofty living standards.

Carey's wife, never totally agreeable to this whole business in the first place, was quick to voice her resentment, to get fed up with their frequent moves to ever more squalid conditions, to fuss with him to his face while he squinted hard to see God's.

"I am in a strange land, alone, no Christian friend, a large family, and nothing to supply their wants. . . . Now all my friends are but one. I rejoice, however, that He is all-sufficient and can supply all my wants, spiritual and temporal."

On days like these, after heading out in search of work but finding no one to trust his motives, after leaving his wife and children in near starvation and returning home with nothing new to feed them, he would uncrumple his wrinkled copy of the farewell sermon his friend Andrew Fuller had preached at Carey's commissioning ceremony. He would remember the last sermon he himself had preached on British soil at the little church in Olney where he had been appointed and ordained into the gospel ministry—a simple message based on the first verse of Romans, chapter twelve.

And he would say to himself in the direst of straits, "Oh! I think again, I am not only ready to be offered, so as to suffer anything, but if I be offered upon the service and sacrifice of the faith, I joy and rejoice in it."

Somehow he was able to see it—the bold inroads he would make into the heart of India, the superstitious souls who would read his translations of the Scriptures in their own dialect and feel unexpected tears pooling in their eyes. He could imagine "desecrating the Ganges River" by baptizing a Hindu believer in waters so often wasted on pagan rituals. He could foresee dozens of schools that would offer the gift of learning and literacy to India's children based on biblical principles. He could dream of a day when the name of Jesus Christ was "no longer strange in this neighborhood."

Of course, he couldn't *really* see it yet—all of these grand accomplishments (and more) that would follow in the years ahead and earn him the undisputed honor of being the "father of modern missions." The great ones in God's sight don't have to see in order to serve. They just have to keep plodding.

As he had said to his nephew and eventual biographer, "If, after my removal, anyone should think it worth his while to write about my life, I will give you a criterion by which you may judge of its correctness. If he gives me credit for being a plodder, he will describe me justly. Anything beyond this will be too much."

His life was on the altar. His only hope was in his Savior.

Plod on.

WHAT'S YOUR STORY?

It's not hard to feel your soul burning for God in the heat of a spiritual moment. But there is a place beyond the glow of the altar—a place as cold and boring and unspiritual as you can imagine—where too many "living sacrifices" discover that their bold promises were just a lot of hot air. Are you willing to remain a light when you honestly don't feel like it?

Psalm 42:1-11 • Matthew 10:34-39 • Luke 17:7-10

AMY CARMICHAEL

If anyone builds on the foundation with gold, silver, costly stones, wood, hay, or straw, each one's work will become obvious, for the day will disclose it; because it will be revealed by fire; the fire will test the quality of each one's work.

—1 Corinthians 3:12-13

AMY CARMICHAEL
GOLDEN OPPORTUNITIES

BELFAST, IRELAND · 1885

Amy Carmichael came into this world at a time when right was right, and wrong was wrong. When there was a place for everything, and everything in its place. When there were certain things that were expected, and certain things that respectable people just didn't do.

Like getting your clothes dirty on a Sunday.

But walking home from church one cheery morning in Belfast, Amy and her brothers spotted a strange sight that called into question all the candor and decorum of Sabbath-keeping. An old woman was shuffling along the shoulder of the street, a heavy bundle of some sort reducing her steps to starts and staggers. How long she had been going, or how far she had yet to go, no one knew . . . or seemed to notice.

It took a moment—between Amy seeing the woman, between looking to see if anyone else saw her seeing her, between the silent "should-we-do-something" that passed between the family—before they broke ranks with the crowd and with custom, and straggled in the direction of helpfulness.

"It meant facing all the respectable people who were, like ourselves, on their way home. It was a horrid moment. We were only two boys and a girl, and not at all exalted Christians. We hated doing it. Crimson all over (at least we felt crimson, soul and body of us) we plodded on, a wet wind blowing us about, and blowing, too, the rags of that poor old woman, till she seemed like a bundle of feathers and we unhappily mixed up with them."

Moving slowly along, they found themselves passing an ornate Victorian fountain—a striking contrast to the tattered spectacle they were creating—when "this mighty phrase was suddenly flashed as it were through the grey drizzle: 'Gold, silver, precious stones, wood, hay, stubble—every man's work shall be made manifest; for the day shall declare it, because it shall be declared by fire; and the fire shall try every man's work of what sort it is. If any man's work abide—' "

Amy turned to see who had said it. No one was there—at least no one who would have spoken such words—only those whose odd stares betrayed the shallowness of their spirituality. But the verse continued tingling in her ears as she and her brothers lugged the bundle and the little old lady along . . . into the distance, nearer her destination.

> "I have been told, 'It is possible to gather gold, where it may be had, by moonlight.' By moonlight, then, let us gather our gold."

Toward a new destiny. A life of disguised, yet golden moments.

Amy wasn't long in looking for them. She soon began having neighborhood girls into her home for prayer and Bible study, which grew to other kinds of meetings at schools and civic centers, and eventually to a class held at the Presbyterian Church for the poor factory girls in town. Most frowned on inviting such untidiness into the church house. Others wondered why Amy's mother would allow her to scour the slums looking for more.

But Amy saw something beautiful in her gathering of outcasts. *There must be something golden there to attract such gossip.*

Within a couple of years, Amy's "Mill Girls' Society" had grown into a full-fledged organization, had erected its own building on a small strip of land,

and was offering a place of hope and joy in the midst of otherwise grinding work and drudgery.

But like others in this book and throughout Christian history, God began placing a "Go ye" calling into Amy's heart. He had gold and silver in other places, yet to be mined. First in Japan. Then in Ceylon. And for the final 50 years of her life . . . in India.

"The pledged word of God to man is no puff-ball to break at a touch and scatter into dust. It is iron. It is gold. It is more golden than gold. It abideth imperishable forever."

Didn't anyone else see the sparkle? "The missionary magazines try to echo the silent sob. You skim them for good stories, nice pictures, bits of excitement—the more the better. Then they drop into the wastepaper basket, or swell some dusty pile in the corner. For perhaps "there isn't much in them." *But to God there is something in it for all that.* Oh! you—you, I mean, who are weary of hearing the reiteration of the great unrepealed commission, you who think you care, but who certainly don't . . . is there *nothing* that will touch you?"

There's gold in those hills. And I'm going over there to get it!

Not that it would be easy to dig up.

More often than not, the Indian people she tried to talk to "scowled and muttered some horrible thing and tottered away. . . .Go! We neither want you nor your book nor your way. . . . Who wants your Lord Jesus here? . . . If I come to him, my devil-god will kill me. Your God is no god. Go tell your lies somewhere else!"

Responses like that went with the territory. Amy knew that coming to Christ in India didn't mean a write-up in the church bulletin but a warrant for your arrest. It meant torture and even death at the hands of your own family. But there were bright spots if you looked for them—if you knew gold when you saw it: one or two children in a little village willing to learn a line of Scripture or sing a gospel song. A woman intrigued by Amy's photographs. An occasional back-and-forth with an educated Hindu.

Yet the treasures that would define her life were the women and girls rescued from "service" to the temple gods. Often they were brought to the shrines as infants—in keeping with some vow or family custom, in exchange for money, in a hundred different ways. They grew up with the official duties of cleaning the building, fanning the image, adding color to the worship experience. But of course, "thanks to the notorious human weaknesses," their jobs invariably degenerated into much more base activities—vile abuses of their femininity—horrors too unthinkable for Amy to confide even to her journals and writings.

Her ministry to them was not intentional at first. It just happened. A seven-year-old girl, who had escaped from the temple once before only to be given back by her mother, her hands branded with hot irons in punishment, somehow slipped out again . . . and somehow (through the protective providence of Someone) ended up at Amy's door.

After this girl would come others, as well as the dangers of being branded a "child stealer." And Amy—stretched in a dozen directions—would be forced to decide whether she and her itinerant band of Christian women should continue their outright evangelism work or "turn from so much that might be profitable and become just nursemaids."

The answer was yes.

"If by doing some work which the undiscerning consider 'not spiritual work' I can best help others, and I inwardly rebel, thinking it is the spiritual for which I crave when in truth it is the interesting and exciting, then I know nothing of Calvary love."

She understood like few others that in order to invest gold in the kingdom of God, sometimes the Sunday clothes must get dirty, the Sunday sentiments must get ruffled, the Sunday occupations must become whatever God places in your hand to do that day.

She had turned her back on wood, hay, and stubble one misty afternoon on an Irish thoroughfare, and "He has kept it as a settled thing in my heart ever since."

Why would anyone settle for less than gold?

WHAT'S YOUR STORY?

A friend once told Amy Carmichael about three inscriptions written over the doors of the cathedral in Milan. One reads, "All that pleases is but for a moment." Another: "All that grieves is but for a moment." And over the great central door: "Nothing is important but that which is eternal." Where have you been sinking your treasure lately—in that which brings pleasure, in that which helps you cling to memories and bitterness, or that which sees today as an investment in forever?

Malachi 3:2-4 • 1 Corinthians 4:1-5 • 1 Peter 1:3-9

JONATHAN EDWARDS

Now to the King eternal, immortal, invisible, the only God, be honor and glory forever and ever. Amen.

—1 Timothy 1:17

JONATHAN EDWARDS
THE BEAUTY OF HOLINESS

NEW HAVEN, CONNECTICUT · 1722

Back near a tangled swamp in the Connecticut woods, where most boys would have gone to hunt squirrels or find trouble, Jonathan Edwards and a few of his childhood pals had built a crude little hideout fashioned with branches and maple leaves. It wasn't a place to play games or store snowballs.

It was a place to pray.

For even early in his life, he had gotten a taste for what it was like to interact with the Almighty—not just in this community prayer closet, but in other secret places outdoors that no one knew about.

And he loved it. Maybe even a little too much. In his Puritan home, where doctrine and theology weren't just Sunday morning sermon topics but daily conversation and dinnertime quizzes, childlike enthusiasm for the faith brought tears of joy to a mama's eyes. Doing good deeds, praying big words, quoting Scripture, and memorizing hymn lyrics earned you enough pats on the back to keep your pride and self-esteem alive for days.

But for all his pious practices—even with the flames of prayerful devotion that drew him out of the house to the birch trees and backwaters—he never seemed to find any peace with God.

In fact, as springlike childhood weathered into young adolescence, the hard-driving God of his staunch, demanding parents seemed less likely to desire his company. The little prayer booth in the woods sat empty, along with a soul losing confidence in a God who seemed to arbitrarily pick and choose the people He liked.

"In process of time, my convictions and affections wore off, and I entirely lost all those affections and delight. I left off secret prayer, at least as to any constant performance of it, and returned like a dog to his vomit, and went on in the ways of sin."

Not the best frame of doubtful mind to go off to college with.

Especially at the tender age of 13.

There—at the Collegiate School of Connecticut (we know it now as Yale University)—this emerging genius in a child's body found himself exposed to the latest philosophies floating through the academic halls. One of them was John Locke's *Essay on Human Understanding*, which secularized Christian teaching by claiming that "the mind is a blank piece of paper" totally formed by experience and perceptions. Edwards gobbled up this exploding world of ideas with more pleasure "than the most greedy miser finds when gathering up handfuls of silver and gold from some newly discovered treasure."

Then unexpectedly in his final year of college, he became suddenly and drastically ill. He was discovered to have pleurisy—a serious swelling around the lungs that made him burn with fever, struggle for even a painful breath, and slip closer to death than a teenager should ever have to come.

"It is no argument against the pleasantness of religion that it has no tendency to raise laughter. . . . The pleasure of religion raises a person clear above laughter, and rather tends to make the face to shine."

By God's grace, he recovered. Yet against God's will, he returned with full health to his old way of life—but this time without the ability to enjoy it.

For months, he wrestled with God, with himself, with his own mind. The Bible's promises from his childhood training pleaded for his first love, yet the restrictions and unfairness they seemed to require stubbornly argued for his common sense.

Until one day he found himself in the Scriptures, reading:

"Now to the King *eternal—immortal—invisible*—the *only* God—be *honor* and *glory*…"

"As I read the words, there came into my soul a sense of the glory of the Divine Being. Never had any words of Scripture seemed to me as these words did. I thought to myself how excellent a Being He was, and how happy I should be if I might enjoy that God, and be wrapped up to Him in heaven, and be swallowed up in Him. I prayed to God that I might *enjoy* Him, and prayed in a manner quite different from what I used to do, with a new sort of affection."

Day by day the gushing fountain of God's grace softened the hard edges of his learning, until Edwards could see for himself that the awesome greatness of

"*Resolved*, constantly, with the utmost diligence and the strictest scrutiny, to be looking into the state of my soul, that I may know whether I have truly an interest in Christ or not; that when I come to die, I may not have any negligence respecting this to repent of."

God could be a delight without being diminished. Knowing that God was in full control could be a comfort, not a curse.

"I seemed to see them both in a sweet conjunction: majesty and meekness joined together—an awful sweetness, a high and great and holy gentleness.

"The appearance of everything was altered. There seemed to be a calm, sweet cast or appearance of divine glory in everything"—both in the dewy spider's web and the thunderstorm, both in the wispy clouds and the crackling lightning. This great mind had been captured by both God's wrath and His rosebuds, and lived to see the peace and power that resides in both.

Indeed, Jonathan Edwards is proof that higher learning can coexist with holy living. He is still considered today (by believers and nonbelievers alike) as a scholar ahead of his time—perhaps even ahead of our modern times—in the vast fields of philosophy, ethics, metaphysics, psychology.

Today's non-Christians see it as a tragic waste that a mind so rich and robust would abandon the lecture halls for the pulpit lectern. They think it a shame that he mingled such stimulating ideas with such archaic theology.

Yet Christians look back with deep admiration on a man whose preaching set off sparks across the New England landscape, inviting holy conviction down from the rafters, sitting people straight up in their seats and forcing them to look squarely into the eyes of eternity. If the historians have it right, some who were on hand to hear his "Sinners in the Hands of an Angry God" sermon clung to the church columns for fear the floor might give way and they'd collapse headlong into hell.

Beginning in his Boston church in the mid-1730s and continuing throughout the country in the 1740s, the Great Awakening ignited both the slumbering church and the average citizen with the compelling claims of the gospel.

Perhaps it helped create the atmosphere that motivated colonial Americans to fight for freedom through the Revolutionary years.

Perhaps it began a Christian heritage in your family going back seven or eight generations.

Perhaps you wouldn't know Christ today if America had not been spared an apathetic nosedive into atheism by the passionate preaching of men like Jonathan Edwards, who taught the world how to find pleasure in the power of God.

WHAT'S YOUR STORY?

Jonathan Edwards loved to sit by his window on stormy nights, marveling at the jagged, flashing sparks of each lightning strike. He knew that the power of this One who flung the thunderbolts also held him safely in the palm of His hand. Read on to join the others who have squinted into the heavens and wondered in awe at the bulging muscles of God's mercy.

Psalm 18:1-19 • John 3:1-17 • 2 Corinthians 3:7-18

JIM ELLIOT

"I am going to send an angel before you to protect you on the road and to bring you to the place that I have prepared."

—Exodus 23:20

JIM ELLIOT
ONE DESIRE

NORMAN, OKLAHOMA · 1950

When most of us think of God calling us to the mission field, to the middle of nowhere, to spartan conditions and suspicious natives, we whisper under our breaths that *surely* He wouldn't do that to us. When a missionary comes to church with his slide show, his snapshots, his snake and spider stories, we can hardly believe that people actually go, that they actually stay, and that they actually like it.

Perhaps that's because we've been seduced by our own habits and luxuries. But just as likely, it's because God has chosen to use us in another outpost of His kingdom—one that's closer to home, nearer to the interests and abilities He's given us. Those He has called into new cultures and climates may at times pine for something more safe and settled, but they go not only because God has said so. They go because they want to. They go because they wouldn't be happy doing anything else.

Duty calls. And desire follows.

Jim Elliot knew that kind of desire. When mentors and classmates marveled at his enthusiastic drive and spiritual insights, imagining what great things he could do for God through his future ministry here in the States, all he wanted to do was to go overseas.

"My going to Ecuador is God's counsel, as is my refusal to be counseled by all who insist I should stay and stir up the believers in the U.S. And how do I know it is His counsel? 'Yea, my heart instructeth me in the night seasons.'

Oh, how good! For I have known my heart is speaking to me for God! No visions, no voices, but the counsel of a heart which desires God."

The Lord had started early on him—around the breakfast table with his brothers and little sister, as his father read from the Scriptures and brought its promising life within full view. His dad being an evangelist, his mom a gracious hostess, they had often opened their home to traveling missionaries, exposing the children to a world beyond their Portland suburb and a purpose beyond all earthly success.

"God, I pray Thee, light these idle sticks of my life and may I burn for Thee. Consume my life, my God, for it is Thine. I seek not a long life, but a full one, like you, Lord Jesus."

At age 20 he had hitchhiked to Mexico with a college friend whose parents were missionaries there. Already the desire was brewing. "Mexico has stolen my heart. We've been here a fortnight (as Ron's folks say; they are very English) and they have invited me to stay as long as I wish. Right now I almost wish it were for life."

Everything was lining up—the pull of foreign missions, a heart for Latin America, the robust beauty of the Spanish language. . . .

The desire to keep following.

"I am as sure of His direction as I am of His salvation."

Ater graduation he went back home to Oregon, working odd jobs, speaking to churches and Christian groups, praying for God to show him the next step . . . which turned out to be a full summer of language training at the University of Oklahoma. Jim's personal tutor there was a former missionary

> *"I know that my hopes and plans for myself could not be any better than He has arranged and fulfilled them. Thus may we all find it, and know the truth of the Word which says, 'He will be our Guide even unto death.'"*

to the Indians of the Ecuadorian jungle—a man whose grasp on the tedious task of transforming an unwritten language into letters on the page was phenomenal. Jim, too, had a sharp mind, and the mechanics of language development rubbed off smoothly from teacher to student. But it was the Indians his teacher had rubbed shoulders with that really brought a knowing sparkle to Jim's eye—an awareness that God had more to reveal to him that summer than the structures of syntax and phonetics.

God's general directions were becoming more specific.

On the Fourth of July, Jim decided it was time to nail this down. He committed himself to ten days of deliberate prayer, "days of vision for me, days wherein are revealed to me those great 'oughts' which must be, if Christ is to have glory." He looked for his answer as he rose in the morning, as he worked through the afternoon, as he buried himself in the Scriptures through the night.

And ten days later, on July 14, 1950, God met him in His Word.

"It came this morning in an unexpected place. I was reading casually in Exodus 23 when verse 20 came out vividly. 'Behold I send an angel before thee to keep thee by the way and to bring thee into the place which I have prepared. Take heed before him.' Coming as it did, with such preceding feelings and such simple believing for some promise, I take this as a leading from God that I should go to Ecuador in the will of God."

• *It was a calling that would cost him his parents' blessing.* Not their blessing, really—just a parent's natural wishes that their children be safe and secure, a steady income beneath their feet and a roof over their heads.

Jim didn't want to worry them, but he couldn't disappoint his heavenly Father. He wrote to his folks: "Remember how the Psalmist described children? He said that they were a heritage from the Lord, and that every man should be happy who had his quiver fill of them. And what is a quiver full of but arrows? And what are arrows for but to shoot? So with the strong arms of prayer, draw the bowstring back and let the arrows fly—all of them, straight at the Enemy's hosts."

• *It was a calling that for a long time would cost him the companionship of a wife.* He had a girlfriend—Betty—but he wrestled mightily with the personal issue of singleness vs. marriage. God's calling for him seemed to require the unencumbered flexibilities of bachelorhood, and it would be three more years—at a time when God needed them to be together in order to fulfill His higher plans—before Jim and his dear Elisabeth were married.

• *And, of course, it was a calling that would cost him his life.* The story is well-known. The savage Auca Indians he and his four friends had attempted to engage mistook their entreaties for treachery, and hacked them to death under a January sky with homemade lances and machetes.

It was a nightmarish end to a God-inspired dream. But for those who go, the obedience that results in death is far more desirable than a disobedience that contents itself with survival.

Four years before, in February 1952, Jim had stood on the deck of the freighter that was carrying him to his eventual South American burial grounds, and had wondered inside why this felt so good. "All the thrill of boyhood dreams came on me just now, watching the sky die in the sea on every side. I wanted to sail since I was in grammar school. . . . Strange—or is it?—that childish hopes should be answered in the will of God.

"I do not understand how God has made me. Joy, sheer joy, and thanksgiving fill and encompass me. I can scarcely keep from saying, 'Brother, this is great!' or 'We never had it so good.' God has done and is doing all I ever desired, much more than I ever asked. Praise, praise to the God of Heaven, and to His Son Jesus. Because He hath said, 'I will never leave thee nor forsake thee,' I may boldly say, 'I will not fear.' "

God had filled him with a desire that even death could not discourage. For the place God had prepared for him to die would become a place where many would find eternal life—even his very killers.

What more can a true believer really want?

WHAT'S YOUR STORY?

Sure, Jim Elliot could have stayed. For many, that is God's calling. To stay. To labor on this shore. There is no shame in that if God has willed it. To go away under those conditions—out of guilt, acclaim, ambition, whatever—would amount to self-righteous disobedience, not sacrifice. With a heart pure before God, you can trust Him to give you not only the directions but also the desire to do His perfect will.

Isaiah 26:3-9 • Romans 1:8-16 • Hebrews 11:13-16

FRANCIS
OF ASSISI

"Don't take along gold, silver, or copper for your money-belts, or a backpack for the road, or an extra shirt, or sandals, or a walking stick, for the worker is worthy of his food."

—Matthew 10:9-10

FRANCIS
OF ASSISI
TO BE LIKE CHRIST

PORTIUNCULA, ITALY · 1209

Francis was born to have everything. But he died before his 45th birthday. With nothing.

And nothing could have suited him better.

He was a man willing to give away all that he had, even stripping to his shorts one day in the palace courtyard—(perhaps stripping even more thoroughly than that!)—in order to show his embarrassed father that he had no more use for high living and fine linen.

God had shown him a better way—a way "more beautiful, more rich, more pure than you could ever imagine." The way of poverty. Friendship with the forsaken. The freedom of neither owning nor being owned by anything.

The freedom to be like Christ.

That's because prestige and possessions look different after you've swapped clothes for the day with a beggar on the streets of Rome, and seen for yourself what it's like to feel insignificant, inhuman, invisible—to those who *have* prestige and possessions.

The hypocrisy of the church appears almost deafening after you've watched men of means come to worship, giving as little in the collection box as their reputations could afford, inspiring in you the indignant decision to add to their pittance every last coin in your change purse.

The needs of others take on new meaning after you've walked voluntarily into a leper hospital, gasped at the stench of rotting flesh, yet have chosen to overcome your aversions, reaching out and embracing one of its chalky victims, kissing him on the cheek, pulling slowly away only to see a lifetime's worth of tears rolling down his empty, cavernous face. "When I was in the bondage of sin," Francis would say, "it was bitter and loathsome to me to look upon those infected with leprosy, but the blessed Lord brought me among them; and when I departed from them, what seemed bitter and loathsome was turned and changed to me into great sweetness and comfort, both of body and soul."

Francis had done all these things. He didn't know why. It didn't match his profile. He had been raised in wealth, had served his country on the battlefield, had spent a year as a prisoner of war, and would have launched into battle again had a fever not sapped his fighting strength.

Why not use such bravery and blueblood to make his own bundle?

It was because of a verse he had heard—for the first time—during Mass one day, a passage that had pricked his ears the moment the priest had read it. Had he heard him right? Francis' Latin wasn't all that great. He could usually make out most of what was being read in church. But unless he had gotten his nouns really turned around, he had heard a lot more than a sentence from Scripture. He had been given a sentence for life.

As soon as the service was over, Francis rushed up to the priest, asking if he would mind reading that verse to him again.

"He abides in a safe place who strives and suffers and works and toils for the Lord God, not through fear of punishment, or for a price, but for love of God."

The priest silently nodded, dutifully turning the heavy pages of the Bible back to the day's reading: the tenth chapter of Matthew. And Francis heard it again—the call of Christ to go into the world without "gold, silver, or copper for your money-belts, or a backpack for the road, or an extra shirt, or sandals, or a walking stick."

Francis stared into the air for several quiet moments, then took a deep breath, turned and looked resolutely into the face of the priest, and said, "Here is what I was looking for. This is what I will do."

And this is what he did: He donned the brown, woolen robe worn by the poorest of the poor in his country, and set out on bare feet to be like Christ to his people. He went into the streets, singing and serving. He wandered into the night, preaching and teaching. He worked—not for money, but for bread—and gave away anything that passed through his hands to those more needy.

> "Grant that I may not so much seek to be consoled as to console; to be understood as to understand, to be loved as to love. For it is in giving that we receive; it is in pardoning that we are pardoned; and it is in dying that we are born to eternal life."

To people living during a time in history when popes were altering passages from the Bible to gain divine sanctions for their powers, when church leaders were too busy with political scrambles to muss their hair over the cares of the common man, when positions of high office were given more on the basis of cash than character,

Francis must have seemed quite out of place as a representative of things spiritual. He had no possessions, no property, no place to lay his head at night, and no desire to start a trend—just a simple man, living a simple life, with the single purpose of being more like Jesus.

The contrast was striking. Yet strangely compelling. Soon there were others falling under the same cloud of conviction, turning their backs on worldly gain to exchange their lives for a greater good. It was nothing official. They had no home or headquarters. They could at best be called a loosely knit brotherhood of like-minded believers, driven to share the Good News of Jesus Christ without the concerns and confinements of home and business.

They taught that union with Christ came not through rites and ceremonies but through a living faith in His gospel, through the daily experience of becoming more like Him in mind, soul, and body. They lived with their hands and hearts what most Christians only spoke with their mouths. They gave when it was costly, suffered when they could have sought shelter, and began each day with an empty slate, waiting for God to fill in the minutes.

When their number had swelled to a dozen, Francis and his followers paid a visit to Rome—to the pope himself—not to lobby for church reform but to offer themselves as its servants. (That was something you didn't hear everyday.) But they were turned away as oddballs. The pope had better things to do than draw up papers for another program.

But by 1219 there were more than 5,000 of them—not because Francis was championing a movement but just because people saw in him a walking witness of Christ's humility and love—a witness that inspired them to be more like Christ themselves. By now there were thousands like him in cities throughout the Western world, earning the trust of people in villages that cared little for the church but loved these selfless servants of Christ.

And now—all of a sudden, and against their will—they seemed to have value to those in high places, too. Couldn't the pope capitalize on this multi-national force of friars to encourage the masses to pay loyalty to him over the king? Couldn't he pull selected men from their number to serve him in other capacities where they'd be more likely than those with family interests to cater to his wishes?

Not on your life, Francis said.

"My friars have been called Minors in order that they not be called Majors. If you desire that they bear fruit in the church, keep them and preserve them in the place to which they were called"—as the servants of Christ, imitating the manner of Christ, pointing those from the lowest rungs of society toward a life in heaven with Christ.

Leave us alone to let us be who we are.

To be like Christ to the world.

WHAT'S YOUR STORY?

Francis endures as a testament to those who have been given an idea by God yet have had no money to do it with, no people to join them, no procedures in place, and no way to work it into their schedule. But those who launch out anyway find that the God who calls also gives the supply—of money, time, companions, whatever. But the only way to know for yourself is simply to obey. See what happens when God takes over.

Ezekiel 2:1-8 • Mark 10:23-31 • Acts 9:10-18

JEROME

"For where your treasure is, there your heart will be also."

—Matthew 6:21

JEROME
HIDDEN TREASURE

ANTIOCH, SYRIA · 374

It is well known that God has chosen to weave some unsavory characters into the fabric of His family. We know about Judah, one of the 12 sons of Jacob, whose lust and loneliness led him to father a child by a young woman he later discovered to be his daughter-in-law. We know about Rahab the prostitute, whose savvy assistance spared the lives of the Israelite spies in Jericho, and knit her tightly enough into the people of God that she became the great-great-grandmother of the great King David.

We've seen God use a talking mule to utter words of spiritual truth at an opportune time. Truth be told, we know a few folks ourselves in the church today who strike us as being more repulsive than regenerate. Yet even though their moods and motivations can clash like plaids and stripes with our own ways of thinking, we somehow share the same faith, the same Lord, the same Savior.

Go figure.

Now let's talk about Jerome—the Jerome who could say to one of his detractors, "Hide your big nose and keep your mouth shut; then you'll appear handsome and an excellent speaker." The Jerome who could accuse a Roman cleric of saying to the poor: "I have not faith and mercy, but such as I have, silver and gold—that I don't give to you either." The Jerome who could never find a way to respond kindly to criticism, yet could always find something *not* to like in just about everyone . . . and every*thing*.

This is one of your brothers in Christ here. A group hug would probably be asking too much.

But the next time you flip through your Bible, you might want to thank the Lord for including this annoyingly articulate hothead in the sheepfold of the saved. Jerome's groundbreaking work in translating the Scriptures helped preserve God's Word for more than a 1,000-year stretch throughout the Middle Ages . . . and in many ways colored the copy you still carry with you to church on Sunday mornings.

You've got to give him this much: He loved to learn.

Virgil, the great Roman poet. Terence, the comic playwright. Sallust, the historian. Cicero, orator and philosopher extraordinaire. Jerome's library bulged with examples of their writings—some purchased with his own money, some painstakingly written out by his own hand, but each of them gathered "with immense zeal and labor" by a man who could bathe in them for hours without coming up for air.

At times his Christian faith peeked its head in, checking to see if he had saved any room for more important things. So on Sundays, Jerome tells us, he and his friends often trekked into the catacombs, visiting the darkened tombs of

"We are destined to know tears before laughter, and to feel grief before joy."

the apostles and martyrs, remembering the price paid by those who died even natural deaths after long lives of Christian obedience.

But on most days, when loneliness would drape around his shoulders, when discouragement would make him question himself and compare his accomplishments with others, when racy, sexual memories would creep into his conscious thoughts, Jerome would always return to his books—the way you or I might flip on a ball game or go for a walk outdoors. He wasn't just reading them for fun but for therapy. For all the wrong reasons. He was clawing at them, tearing ravenously at their pages, yet sensing the painful inadequacy of only being able to read one page at a time.

Yes, he believed in Christ. In fact, his compulsive nature had caused him to crave not only ordinary obedience but the sacrificial pains of severe discipleship—the fastings, the quiet, the rigors of non-stop repentance.

> "Make knowledge of the Scripture your love, and you will not love the vices of the flesh. Live with them, meditate on them, make them the sole object of your knowledge and inquiries."

But his ideals were constantly tripping over his treasure chest—his love for the pagan classics.

Until one night in 374.

Jerome had left his hometown two years prior, his family rejecting his obnoxious airs and his big Christian talk. When he finally found some believers in northern Italy who shared his desire for deep devotion, he quickly succeeded in offending them too with his cruel criticisms and biting tongue. With no more use for their company, and thinking that maybe a visit to the Holy Land might cure his wild temptations and wanderlust, he headed east . . . but only made it as far as Antioch before sickness slowed his pace and confined him to his quarters at the home of an old acquaintance.

And that's where it happened. Asleep in bed after another day of disappointment and dissatisfaction, he dreamed that he was being called to approach the bench in a heavenly courtroom. His heart raced. Cold sweat tingled on his forehead. Walking too slowly to suit the Judge, he sensed himself being dragged by meaty arms to the base of the tribunal, where dazzling light melted the muscles in his knees and he collapsed in terror.

Suddenly a booming voice thundered that he *identify himself!*

Jerome's words came out meekly, mousily: "I . . . I am a Christian."

"You are lying!" the Judge roared without a pause. "You are a disciple of Cicero, not of Christ; for your heart is where your treasure is."

The rest of the dream flew by with flashes of light and the snap of bullwhips. In fact, Jerome was still crying aloud for mercy when he awoke—his lungs heaving, his eyes white, his room spinning. Before the floor could rise to meet him, he fell from his bedside, crying into trembling hands, "Lord, if ever again I possess worldly books, if ever I read them, I shall have denied You!"

I want You for my treasure! I want You with all my heart!

So with his nose free from the pages of half-truths, he embarked on a new quest of understanding—the ancient Hebrew tongue of the Old Testament. He had no dictionaries, no grammar books, no study aids to help him. If that didn't make it challenging enough, he found the written Hebrew language to be made up of nothing but consonants! Many times he threw down his work, convinced it was beyond him. But God would dangle the treasure of His Word before Jerome's eyes, and he would return to his desk with new zest and vigor.

So when years later he returned to Rome, and was requested by the pope himself to begin a new translation of the Psalms into Latin, he knew right where to go—beyond the Greek manuscripts, to the original language, to his new treasure. By the early part of the fifth century, he had completed the entire Old Testament. And with the help of a few others who finished his thorough revision of the New Testament after his death, the Latin Vulgate became the universal Bible of Western Christianity for generations.

One thousand years later, when John Wycliffe began translating the Bible into English—the common language of his people—he used the Latin Vulgate as his template. Two hundred years after that, when Martin Luther began translating the Bible into German—the common language of *his* people—he used the Latin Vulgate as his starting point.

So call Jerome whatever you want to. Gruff. Narrow. Vindictive. Mean. But underneath all that blow and bluster, Jerome had found life's truest treasure in the ancient Scriptures.

And somewhere in the mysteries of God, we discover the grace to call him our friend.

WHAT'S YOUR STORY?

Outside of your daily work and responsibilities, what activities get the best hours of your day? The evening news? Smutty sitcoms? Sports talk? Video games? Oprah? If the Bible consistently fails to measure up to the thrill and enjoyment of the competition, you can be sure the problem is not with the Scripture's power but with your own priorities. Have you tried staying in the Word long enough lately to see what a wonder your God really is?

Psalm 19:7-11 • Proverbs 8:1-11 • Ecclesiastes 1:12-18

ADONIRAM JUDSON

"Go, therefore, and make disciples of all nations, baptizing them in the name of the Father and of the Son and of the Holy Spirit."

—Matthew 28:19

ADONIRAM JUDSON

STAR IN THE EAST

ANDOVER, MASSACHUSETTS · 1809

Night wasn't the only thing falling on young Adoniram Judson that late September evening in the Massachusetts countryside. So were his dreams of making his mark on the New York stage as a shooting-star playwright and actor. So was his brash confidence that the brilliance he had shown in the world of big ideas at Brown University could help him handle anything the real world could throw at him. So were his plans for what to do with his life the next day, and the next, as he aimlessly drifted away from the city, away from home and parents in Rhode Island—just away.

Tired, confused, dejectedly drawing his horse toward the light of a roadside inn, he entered to find that only one room remained vacant for the night—and a disclaimer even on that one. The young man staying in the room next to his was critically ill and in excruciating pain—dying, actually. *It might be hard to get much sleep*, the innkeeper said.

Judson didn't care. He wasn't afraid of the sights and sounds of death. Nor of God, if there was one—especially if He was the sour, humorless God of his Puritan preacher-father. Judson was an educated man now, comfortable in his faithlessness. Comfortable enough to doze while another man died.

But nothing prepared him for the agonies of that night—the grimacing cries of his dying neighbor, the frantic gasps for breath, the nearness of death that hung in the midnight air over Judson's bed and made him ask questions he had long dismissed as fantasies: *What would happen to this man's soul on the other side of death—this "young man" the innkeeper had described? And even more chilling: What would I be facing tonight if I were dying instead of him?*

This wasn't the way they had drawn it up on the board at Brown. He and his buddies John Bailey and (especially) Jacob Eames had scoffed at the idea of an actual heaven and hell, of a personal God that welcomed you to His side or a literal devil that seethed with sinister pleasure upon your arrival. *What would those guys think if they knew what I was thinking now?*

Sleep came. Finally. And within hours the sunlight streaming through the draperies had dispelled the nightmarish worries of the night. So when Judson stepped into the lobby that morning, some of that snobbish confidence was back as he casually asked the innkeeper what had become of the guest in the room next door. Sure enough, poor soul, the man had died during the night.

An awkward pause.

"Do you know who he was?" Judson heard himself break the silence, though why this mattered or why he cared he didn't really know.

"Yes, he was a young man from the college at Providence. Name was Jacob Eames."

Jacob Eames? The classmate who had been the loudest voice to laugh Judson and others into near atheism? The big-talking Brown grad with the world on a leash and God in a box?

"Suffering and success go together. If you are succeeding without suffering, it is because others before you have suffered. If you are suffering without succeeding, it is so that others after you may succeed."

The news sent Judson reeling for home, reeling for answers. Alert but still questioning, he received special permission to enter Andover Theological Seminary without declaring himself a candidate for the ministry or even a Christian. But he wasn't long in the presence of truth before God made the way clear to Judson's mind. On December 2, 1808, he "began to entertain a hope of having received the regenerating influences of the Holy Spirit" and "made a solemn dedication of himself to God."

And within a year, his newfound faith had given his life a whole new direction.

"I am not tired of my work, neither am I tired of the world. Yet when Christ calls me home, I shall go with the gladness of a boy bounding away from his school."

In September 1809 he came across a printed sermon entitled "The Star in the East." The message told of the gospel's impact in India, as believers from Great Britain, Germany, and other European nations had crossed land and sea to take God's Word to the East.

But why were *Americans* not looking beyond their own shores, their own pulpits, their own noses? "They let three-fourths of the world sleep the sleep of death, ignorant of the simple truth that a Savior died for them. Content to be useful in the little circle of their acquaintances, they quietly sit and see whole nations perish for lack of knowledge."

God was calling him away, all right—not north to the city theatre, not south to a Boston pastorate, not west to the university lecture hall. He was calling him east. *Far* East.

"It was during a solitary walk in the woods behind the college, while meditating and praying on the subject, and feeling half inclined to give it up, that the command of Christ, 'Go into all the world and preach the gospel to every creature,' was presented to my mind with such clearness and power, that I came to a full decision. And though great difficulties appeared in my way, I resolved to obey the command at all events."

It was a calling that would require visionary faith. For example, no American missionary board existed to send men and women overseas with support, contacts, and game plans. So Judson and a handful of others who were sharing a similar burden for the souls of the world organized one themselves. But while translating the Scriptures during his voyage across the Atlantic, he was convinced that the baptism practices of his sending church were unbiblical. So although he left America as a Congregationalist, he arrived in India as a Baptist—and found himself cut off from even the feeble support of his own fledgling missionary society.

His bride of less than a month would write, "We have endeavored to count the cost, and be prepared for the many severe trials resulting from this change of sentiment. We anticipate the loss of reputation, and of the affection and esteem of many of our American friends. We feel that we are alone in the world, with no real friend but each other, no one on whom we can depend but God."

But his calling to "go into all the world" would cost them more than money and reputation.

Three of their children would die from disease. Driven from Calcutta, they would move even farther east to Burma, and labor for six long years among the stench and squalor of its hopeless, heathen mission fields before the gospel would win its first convert there.

When war broke out between the British and the Burmese, Judson was tagged as a British spy and treated to greater cruelty than perhaps any other person in the annals of Christian missions—chained by the ankles to a bamboo pole that was lifted above his head at night, forcing him to swing suspended by his neck and shoulders, driven barefoot for miles through the fiery sands of the Eastern desert until the blistered skin tore away from the soles of his feet, starved to emaciation and tortured by daily 3 p.m. executions of his fellow prisoners. On a few occasions, with his wife nearby and weakened by meningitis, he would be released to walk the streets in search of any Burmese mother who could nurse his infant daughter.

But somehow God gave him strength—even during his 18 months of cruel confinement—to continue and finally complete his translation of the entire Bible in the Burmese language. And though his wife died much too young from fevers and tropical illness, he dealt with his grief by returning to his work. Before his death in 1850, he led more than 7,000 to Christ, establishing dozens of churches and blazing the trail as the first American missionary on foreign soil.

For God had called him as a light to the world, and his life became a shining star in the East.

WHAT'S YOUR STORY?

Perhaps the call of God is lining up in your own life—an unmistakable pull in one direction, a thought that won't go away, a theme that keeps cropping up. You may not know what you ought to do next. You may not be sure you're up to the challenge. But sometimes the biggest challenge in doing God's will is realizing that you can't do it—that it will take God Himself to do it through you.

Isaiah 6:1-8 • Acts 20:17-37 • 1 Corinthians 2:1-5

MARTIN LUTHER KING, JR.

"You have heard that it was said, 'You shall love your neighbor and hate your enemy.' But I tell you, love your enemies, and pray for those who persecute you."

—Matthew 5:43-44

MARTIN LUTHER KING, JR.

LOVE YOUR ENEMIES

MONTGOMERY, ALABAMA · 1955

"Do to us what you will, and we will still love you.

"Bomb our homes and threaten our children, and as difficult as it is, we will still love you. Send your hooded perpetrators of violence into our communities at the midnight hour, drag us out on some wayside road and leave us half-dead as you beat us, and we will still love you. Send your propaganda agents around the country and make it appear that we are not fit, culturally and otherwise, for integration, and we will still love you.

"We shall match your capacity to inflict suffering by our capacity to endure suffering, and we will win our freedom."

If it were anyone else talking, you'd swear those were fighting words. And over the years, in the frustrating battle for racial justice and equality, many would indeed resort to rocks, bricks, and violence to express their righteous outrage.

But read those opening sentences again. Locate the theme—the one word—that dominates the message. And reconsider.

Those are the words of love.

Martin Luther King understood that love at its highest level transcended pleasant conversation. Love had more teeth in it than your basic smile. Love was hard work. Love hurt. But love was freedom—the freedom to stare back into the bloodshot, blood-seeking eyes of human hatred and see a creature God had fashioned with His own hands, a person in dire need of His redemption, a man shouting slogans he didn't really understand. "We must never let up in our determination to remove every vestige of segregation and discrimination from this country, but we shall not in the process relinquish our privilege to love."

The cause was just. He was sure it would one day take his people where they wanted to go.

But only if love did the driving.

"Our aim must be not to defeat or humiliate the white man, but to win his friendship and understanding. We must never become bitter, nor should we succumb to the temptation of using violence in the struggle, for if this happens, unborn generations will be the recipients of a long and desolate night of bitterness, and our chief legacy to the future will be an endless reign of meaningless chaos."

"Power at its best is love implementing the demands of justice. Justice at its best is love correcting everything that stands against love."

It almost was.

Late in his short life, the tone of the civil rights movement began taking a sharp turn to the right. Many of the new, more youthful leaders had decided that change was moving too slowly, progress was being corrupted by compromise, turning the other cheek was getting them nowhere. Even some of the ones most loyal to King and his nonviolent methods were starting to burn low in the patience department, ready to bust some heads. No more Mr. Nice Guy. It was fast becoming Black Power payback time.

But they didn't know power the way Martin Luther King knew it. He knew a power greater than guns and bullets, a force more deadly than blue-streak swearing and switchblades.

He knew the power of love. And he had seen it kill a lot of bad things.

He had watched it bring prejudice to its knees in Montgomery, Alabama, after a year-long bus boycott put the world on notice that racial discrimination was entering its death cycle. He had watched it topple the bigoted brass in Birmingham's city hall and earn African-Americans a seat at the table in the city's all-white lunchrooms and libraries. He had watched it march through ranks of armed troopers in the little town of Selma, Alabama, and turn thousands of second-class citizens into duly registered voters.

Of course, "the privilege to love" had come with the accompanying privilege of spending long nights in jail, scraping egg yolks from the face, and being chased off the sidewalk with fire hoses, tear gas, and police dogs. It had meant broken arms and bloody noses, knees to the groin and bottles to the head. Too often it had ended in death—sometimes at the hands of those sworn to protect the public.

But King looked back to the movement's roots—and farther back to the movement's inspiration—and determined that the price of love was always worth paying.

He wrote: "From the beginning a basic philosophy guided the movement. This guiding principle has since been referred to variously as nonviolent resistance, noncooperation, and passive

"I've seen too much hate to want to hate, myself. I've seen hate on the faces of too many sheriffs and too many Klansmen to want to hate, myself. And every time I see it, I say to myself, hate is too great a burden to bear."

resistance. But in the first days of the protest none of these expressions was mentioned; the phrase most often heard was 'Christian love.'

"It was the Sermon on the Mount, rather than a doctrine of passive resistance, that initially inspired the Negroes of Montgomery to dignified social action. It was Jesus of Nazareth that stirred the Negroes to protest with the creative weapon of love.

"In a world in which most men attempt to defend their highest values by the accumulation of weapons of destruction, it was morally refreshing to hear five thousand Negroes in Montgomery shout 'Amen' and 'Hallelujah' when they were exhorted to 'pray for those who oppose you,' or pray 'Lord, give us strength of body to keep walking for freedom,' and conclude each meeting with: 'Let us pray that God shall give us strength to remain nonviolent, though we may face death.' "

But sadly, it took a death—his own death—to show that violence can never accomplish what love can.

On April 4, 1968, when a sniper's bullet claimed King's life on a Memphis motel balcony, the tensions that had threatened to boil over into new battles and bloodshed suddenly caught in the collective throat of the civil rights movement. One of the men who had pushed harder than most to force King out of his nonviolent ways said, "He was the one man in our race who was trying to teach us to have love, compassion, and mercy for white people."

And now he was gone, having been labeled too weak by some of his own, and labeled names too profane to print by most of his enemies. To friend and foe alike, he was nothing if not extreme.

"Though I was initially disappointed at being categorized as an extremist, as I continued to think about the matter, I gradually gained a measure of satisfaction from the label. Was not Jesus an extremist for love? 'Love your enemies, bless them that curse you, do good to them that hate you, and pray for them which despitefully use you and persecute you.' So the question is not whether we will be extremists, but what kind of extremists we will be.

"In that dramatic scene on Calvary's hill, three men were crucified. Two were extremists for immorality and thus fell below their environment. Jesus Christ was an extremist for love, truth, and goodness, and thereby rose above His environment. Perhaps the South, the nation, and the world are in dire need of creative extremists."

He had found his *Words to Die For.*

WHAT'S YOUR STORY?

One of the first rules of both the ballfield and the battlefield is to know your enemy, to understand his motives, to anticipate the way he'll react in given situations. We're all pretty good at that: We know who our enemies are, and we never let them forget it. But Jesus doesn't say anything about knowing our enemies. He just talks about loving them. What does that look like in your life . . . with your enemies?

Luke 10:25-37 • Acts 7:54-60 • Romans 12:14-21

JOHN KNOX

"I have given them Your word. The world hated them because they are not of the world, just as I am not of the world."

—John 17:14

JOHN KNOX
DISTANT THUNDER

ST. ANDREWS, SCOTLAND · 1545

John Knox's heroes were dropping like flies in 16th-century Scotland.

First it was Patrick Hamilton, burned at the stake in St. Andrews for teaching doctrines opposed to church policy. Given a chance to recant, he declared that he was "not in awe of your fire," that he considered a short time in the flames a fair trade in order to avoid hell's furnace for all eternity. Little did he know that his ordeal that day would seem like an eternity. If you've ever watched a British Open golf tournament from the storied Old Course in this ancient city, you've seen the fierce winds whip the players' pantlegs and carry their nimblest approach shots waist-deep into the weeds. Imagine trying to get a good fire going in one of those chilly gales howling off the North Sea. Hamilton roasted for six hours that day, the woodpile being several times restacked and relighted, but he never resorted to a retraction. He raised his blackened hands in praise to God, and set the stage for the Reformation of Scotland.

Then it was George Wishart, a Protestant preacher whose knack for persuasion had caught the wily eyes of those who saw in him a pawn for their political aims. They hoped to harness his appeal and passion to help break the hold of Rome on the throne of Scotland. But between the archbishop in Edinburgh and the cardinal who had declared himself Scotland's ruler, Wishart never stood a chance in the kangaroo court that convicted him of sedition. When the executioner saw the humble dignity and demeanor of this unworthy criminal, he fell to his knees to beg Wishart's understanding for having to carry out his duty. Wishart reached down, kissed the executioner on the cheek, and told him he was forgiven.

And next in line would be John Knox—not to burn a path to glory in the town square, but to be hated and reviled his entire life by those who detested everything he stood for.

Some martyrs have to *live* their sentence.

But Knox's was really more than a sentence. It was a whole chapter—the Gospel of John, chapter seventeen.

He first came across this passage as a young teacher, fresh out of the university, prepared for a life of inconspicuous service to his nation, his government, his church.

But in the lines of Jesus' high priestly prayer for His disciples, Knox saw for the first time that the true church of Christ was not the great machine he saw around him, the church that held people in its suffocating grip, but an invisible church held in the loving, caring, all-sufficient hands of the One who gave it birth, sustained its life, and won for it a hope more permanent than death.

This is not a slam against the Catholic Church. No one today—Catholic or Protestant—would call the medieval church anything else but what it was: a fat, corrupt, indecent imitation of everything God intended His Bride on earth to be. Its leaders stripped whole nations

"Our kingdom, our joy, our rest and happiness neither was, is, nor should be in the earth, or in any transitory thing, but in heaven, into which we must enter by many tribulations."

"If you desire your knowledge to be increased, your faith to be confirmed, your conscience to be quieted and comforted, let your exercise be frequent in the law of the Lord."

of their wealth, sired children out of wedlock with its most beautiful women, and never batted an eye at any directive from Rome, no matter how greedy or ungodly. The popes themselves were at times not just indifferent to Christianity but aggressively opposed to it. A few good ones came along, tossed very infrequently into the mix, but most of them—as well as the army of cardinals, bishops, and priests that served their wishes throughout the Empire—were more in love with gain and power than with God and His people.

And perhaps nowhere in the world was the church worse than in John Knox's Scotland.

But the Scots were—and still are—an independent bunch. Enraged by Wishart's death at the hands of a pretend ruler, a band of rebels stormed the castle and put the cardinal's body on ice. Among their number were some of the fathers of Knox's students, who asked him to move to the now besieged castle and become their chaplain. He reluctantly accepted. But when the castle finally fell to French military pressure, Knox found himself guilty by association and spent the next year and a half chained to an oar as a galley slave.

With plenty of time to think.

He thought about his precious, precarious Scotland. He thought about its people, his family, his neighbors, chained like him to an impersonal system that frustrated their freedoms and disregarded their faith. He thought about

John 17, about a church known only to Christ, a church that had no quarter in the world and no rest from its enemies, a church that had no desire for earthly pleasures but an insatiable hunger for the truth of God's Word.

When his captors' vessel sailed along the coast of Scotland, Knox could see the old, familiar landmarks through the few openings in the ship's belly. If the boat's position was just right, he could even spot the steeple top of the parish church where he had preached to his renegade flock. Oh, if he should ever get out of here alive, what he wouldn't give to again "glorify that godly name in the same place" where he had declared it so often before.

In time he would be freed. In time he would preach again in the heart of his homeland. But it would happen in the most roundabout of ways.

First, he headed for England, where he pushed for Protestant reforms under the agreeable reign of Edward VI. But Edward would die too young, and Mary Tudor would take his place—"Bloody Mary," who stamped out the fires of reform by putting hundreds to death and making refugees out of anyone who eluded her fiery grasp.

Knox was one who escaped. He ended up in Geneva, Switzerland, during John Calvin's heyday, and pastored the faithful who had bolted there from Britain. Yet his eyes would ever burn for Scotland. Thirteen years after being dragged away as a slave, he finally returned for good to push his nation's ruthless leaders over the brink. "I see the battle shall be great, for Satan rages to the uttermost; and I am come (I praise my God) even into the brunt of the battle. Pray that I shrink not when the battle approaches."

He personified the conscience of a mighty civil war, a national uprising for religious freedom. Isolated and outnumbered, his puny ranks appeared a finger-flick from defeat against the royal army and the French who stood behind them. The queen would ask in fiendish glee, "Where is John Knox's God now?" But Knox rallied the unlikely support of England to his side, and the queen ran for her life.

Still, the fight was far from over. Though he had won the day in Parliament, Knox now had a new queen to deal with: Marie Stuart—Mary, Queen of Scots—herself a loyal servant of Rome. She warned him that he would not always be free to lead his people in worship, that she would have her revenge for his insinuations that she somehow owed her high position to his hideous God. But under her breath she would mutter, "I fear the prayers of John Knox more than all the assembled armies of Europe." And before her reign could come to full flower, her head would fall into an English executioner's basket.

Scotland was free. And John Knox was its liberator. Yet he knew full well that Christ alone was the champion of Scottish reform. Even on his deathbed, barely able to summon enough strength to speak, Knox called for someone to read his favorite passages . . . especially John 17, "the place where I cast my first anchor."

The place where he first heard the thunder of another world. And gave his life so that others could hear it, too.

WHAT'S YOUR STORY?

Do you find yourself judging too harshly those who sometimes resort to rudeness in order to express their deeply held convictions? Jesus could be rude. I don't know what else you'd call his tirades against the entrenched religious authorities of His day. Some people (like John Knox) need no invitation in order to be blunt. But maybe you do. Are you willing to offend if that's what it takes to offer your friends freedom from their sins?

Jeremiah 5:20-31 • Matthew 23:33-39 • Galatians 1:6-10

DAVID LIVINGSTONE

"And remember, I am with you always, to the end of the age."

—Matthew 28:20

DAVID
LIVINGSTONE
NEVER ALONE

ZAMBEZI RIVER, AFRICA · 1856

It was settled. He was going to China. He was going to save enough money to put himself through medical school, get as much education as he could, then apply to the London Missionary Society as a full-time journeyman.

That was the plan.

But he hadn't planned on a war breaking out in the East. So with his papers on hold and his commission postponed, he waited. And worked. And wondered what he was going to do with all this drive and energy . . . and nowhere to go with it.

To fill the time on one of those restless days, he attended a meeting led by Dr. Robert Moffat, fresh from his missionary work in Kuruman, South Africa—500 miles inland, the deepest point anyone had yet reached with the gospel. And wow! The savagery. The sacred rituals. The dangers of daily life on the Dark Continent.

But more than the exotic tales of wild beasts and poison arrows, Dr. Moffat made one poetic statement that grabbed young David Livingstone by the shoulders and turned him a full forty degrees to the southeast . . . to face a new frontier: "I have sometimes seen in the morning sun the smoke of a thousand villages, where no missionary has ever been."

Now it was settled. He was going to Africa.

But when he finally got there—by steamer and ox-wagon—he wasn't content just to *watch* the smoke rise from the nearby huts and hovels. He wanted to smell it, taste it, perhaps be the one to help kindle the cooking fire and sit down to visit with the tribesmen, to experience their customs, to learn their language. So instead of staying close to the missionary compound, venturing out only when it was reasonably safe, he relocated to a nearby village and pitched camp next door to the natives.

At night when they swapped stories about mysterious gods and ancient heroes, he would tell them about the one true God, the hero of all mankind. When the villagers praised him for attacking a wild beast that threatened the lives of their children, he showed them his bloodied fingers and told them of a God-man who spilled His blood to save children of all nations from death. As they watched their dying friends and family brought back to their feet by one of Livingstone's treatments or medicines, he would tell them of a God with the power to heal both body and soul.

And they responded. He wrote home to his father, "The work of God goes on here notwithstanding all our infirmities. Souls are being gathered continually. Twenty-four were added to the church last month."

That's because Livingstone's view of missionary duty was not like those "whose ideal is a dumpy sort of man with a Bible under his arm." To be sure, he enjoyed nothing more than "preaching the unsearchable riches of Christ, for it always warms my heart." The gospel of grace was never silent when he was around. But for him the missionary call included "laboring in bricks and mortar,

"Good and gracious Jesus, Thou art ever near. Thou knowest my yearnings after these people. Thou art my comfort and my keeper. Stay with me, Lord, till my work is done."

at the forge and the carpenter's bench." He considered that he was "serving Christ when shooting a buffalo for my men or taking an astronomical observation." Or exploring uncharted territory for signs of fresh vegetation and water supplies. Or seeking to establish clear trade routes to the ocean so foreign merchants would seek the land's natural riches instead of its slave labor.

> "May they not forget the pioneers who worked in the thick gloom with few rays to cheer, except such as flow from faith in the precious promises of God's Word."

It's the kind of calling that can kill a man if he's not careful. Eventually, it would.

It's the kind of calling that can make your financial supporters wonder if you're doing missionary business or just enjoying your nature studies. And it would one day cost him their approval and backing.

It's the kind of calling that can put you at javelin-point while passing through jungle lands where warlords and headhunters rule by blood and distrust.

And it was on that kind of night, deep in the unknown, unmapped heart of Africa, desperately seeking a path to the sea that would bring his adopted continent within reach of the world, that David Livingstone called to mind a verse of Scripture that towered above his darkest, deadliest fears.

On this night even his tribal companions were jittery and suspicious. The dense, muggy air was thick with anxiety. Screeches. Snapped branches. Sleeplessness. He wrote in his journal: "I felt much turmoil of spirit in view of having all my plans for the welfare of this great region knocked on the head by savages tomorrow. But I read that Jesus came and said, 'All power is given unto me in heaven and in earth. Go ye therefore, and teach all nations—and lo (*this next part was underlined*), I am with you alway, even unto the end of the world.' This is the word of a gentleman of the most sacred and strictest honor.

"I will not cross furtively by night as I intended. It would appear as flight. Why should such a man as I flee? No, I shall take my observations for latitude and longitude tonight, though they may be the last.

"I feel quite calm now, thank God."

Calm? There was no calmness in the nearby village, where the bloodthirsty natives were warning their wives and children to stay away from the riverbank the next morning. Armed and vigilant, they crept into position to surround the expedition party at sunrise, to stain the waters of the Zambezi with flowing blood.

Yet the travellers and their white-man doctor awoke with a quiet serenity that stunned and stymied the savages. While Livingstone made gestures of peace, letting them listen to the ticking of his pocketwatch, showing them how to ignite a flame with the lens of his magnifying glass, his companions glided their belongings onto canoes and safely across the river. By the time Livingstone had boarded as the final passenger, his enemies were sending him off with smiles and waves . . . as friends.

God had been with him—even at the far end of the earth—turning strangers into brothers. Turning fear into freedom. Turning death into life.

It would happen over and over again in Livingstone's Africa.

That's why on his first trip home after 16 dangerous years away, with his published journals earning him superstar status—with book sales comfortably setting him up for life in his Scottish homeland if he wanted—he could stand on the podium to receive his honorary doctorate from the University of Glasgow and say, "I return to Africa without misgiving and with gladness of heart. For would you like me to tell you what supported me through all my years of exile among people whose attitude toward me was always uncertain and often hostile?

"It was this: 'Lo, I am with you alway, even unto the end of the world.' On those words I staked everything, and they have never failed! I was never left alone!"

Even to the end.

Early one morning several years later, one of his African friends peered into Livingstone's hut to see what was keeping him from the day's work. There he was, kneeling by his bedside, head down, hands folded.

An hour passed. Then two. Worried that something was wrong, the man crept quietly into his room only to find Livingstone dead—his body still at prayer. He had passed into glory in the arms of his heavenly companion, leaving Africa with a future, leaving wild men with a witness.

And never having known a day when he was left alone.

WHAT'S YOUR STORY?

In some stretches of life, we foolishly think that we can do without God's presence, exchanging it for the companionship of casual friends and comfortable sins. They seem more pleasurable, less demanding. But (don't we all know) they leave a lonely aftertaste. Must life get hard, must friends get few, must the years get by before we realize that His presence alone is our only source of lasting joy and protection?

1 Kings 8:22-30 • Psalm 16:1-11 • John 16:22-33

MARTIN LUTHER

God's righteousness is revealed from faith to faith, just as it is written: "The righteous will live by faith."

—Romans 1:17

MARTIN
LUTHER
FAITH COMES TO LIFE

WITTENBURG, GERMANY · 1517

All was quiet in his tower room. Everywhere but in his own soul.

And his soul was mad at God.

It wasn't the anger of a hardened sinner, spitting blasphemies at a God he wished would go away. He wanted to please God more than he wanted anything in his life! Why else had he often clawed away at his own flesh, pounding his body with a closed fist over the slightest offense? He had burned so many paths to the confession box, they had begged him to quit coming back. *You're being too hard on yourself. You're worried about things most people don't even notice!*

"But I, blameless monk that I was, felt that before God I was a sinner with an extremely troubled conscience. I couldn't be sure God was pleased by my apologies." No matter how much confessing, no matter how much sorrow, no matter how many times he kicked himself for thinking an unkind thought—or wishing he didn't have to study—or picking up the wrong fork—this God never let up!

What's a man to do?

"Isn't it enough that we miserable sinners, lost for all eternity because of original sin, are oppressed by every kind of calamity through the Ten Commandments? Why does God heap sorrow upon sorrow through the gospel [of all places] and threaten us with His justice and wrath?"

Day and night this went on. While the world helped themselves to immorality, while the church elite dined on wealth and luxury, this humble teacher tortured himself over the mildest of mistakes. And God, so it seemed, was unmoved by his guilt. Luther never felt a moment's peace, an hour's rest, or an afternoon's enjoyment. His best was always inadequate, his effort never enough. Most days were depressing, most nights long and fitful.

But in the middle of his grumblings one evening, with Paul's letter to the Romans spread before him as he prepared his biblical lectures, God mercifully pulled back the blinders and pieced together both halves of Romans 1:17 in Luther's mind.

Yes, "the justice of God" was still there—the righteous purity of a God who demanded holy, flawless perfection from His creatures. But so was this adjoining phrase: "The just shall live by faith."

"Shall *live?*"

He almost laughed. The life Martin Luther had experienced hardly felt like living—working like crazy to get God to like him, but stumbling over his own failure and faithlessness at every turn.

Where was this *life* Paul was talking about?

"Faith is a living, bold trust in God's grace, so certain of God's favor that it would risk death a thousand times trusting in it."

It was found in putting both halves together—the righteousness of God and the faith of God's people—and watching them add up to lasting joy. It wasn't about how well Martin Luther could perform, but about a grace that had already done all the work.

Luther's pen dropped to the floor. He had never thought of this before. Never had he seen God's face that it wasn't dark, dour, disapproving. But suddenly—a smile. A God who is satisfied. A God who nods His head and is pleased with what He sees. Through the mercy of the cross, working through the faith of the believer, God's demands for justice have been met.

Christians can . . . *live.*

"All at once I felt that I had been born again and entered into paradise itself through open gates. Immediately I saw the whole of Scripture in a different light. I exalted this sweetest word of mine—the justice of God—with as much love as before I had hated it."

> "Faith cannot help doing good works constantly. It doesn't stop to ask if good works ought to be done, but before anyone asks, it already has done them and continues to do them without ceasing. . . . It is just as impossible to separate faith and works as it is to separate heat and light from fire!"

Knowing the Scriptures like he did, he sprinted through them by memory:

- "The strength of God" wasn't a sledgehammer to beat him to death, but the source of his own strength.

- "The power of God" wasn't a whip to punish his every move, but a gift to make him powerful.

- "The wisdom of God" wasn't a peering librarian who scolded him for what he was thinking, but divine knowledge revealed to him in order to make him wise.

- "The righteousness of God" wasn't a weapon but a gift—a holiness so pure, it made even the nastiest sinner who trusted in Christ look good in God's eyes.

Luther could wipe the sweat off

his guilt complex. He could crank down his nerve settings from *panic* to *peace*. He could live his holy life but realize that his good deeds weren't brownie points on God's scoreboard.

He could . . . *live.*

But he also knew he couldn't keep it to himself. If people were to be free to experience God's salvation through faith alone, the shady practices and shoddy theology of the church in his day had to be faced down and stopped. Standing up against it would be like storming the castle with nickels and thumbtacks. But somebody had to do it.

And that somebody was Martin Luther.

So he took the weapons of pen and paper (and hammer and nails) and pounded his complaints onto the cathedral door in Wittenburg (sort of a 16th-century version of an internet bulletin board). These *95 Theses*— blistering accusations against church corruption and conceit—not only scarred the wood finish but exposed the raw flesh of longstanding traditions that had been scaring people into submission and selling God's forgiveness to the highest bidder.

Within months, Luther was a German folk hero. Through lectures and debates, he had jabbed his finger to the chest of a self-serving church system that was draining money and morale from well-meaning people, and he had rallied the emerging masses to his side.

Angry popes notice things like that. And they notice them very persuasively.

In 1520 Luther was excommunicated from the church. And in 1521 he was ordered to appear in court before the emperor himself. But pressed to renounce his views, Luther stood his ground: "My conscience is captive to the Word of God. Thus I cannot and will not recant, for going against my conscience is neither safe nor beneficial. I can do no other. Here I stand. God help me."

And with that, the Protestant Reformation was in full swing, running at full stride.

His faith had found a resting place. And it would live to shake the world.

WHAT'S YOUR STORY?

You don't want to know how many sins you commit in a day. It would scare you. Even the good things you do are gummed up with bits and pieces of selfishness. But if you're a believer in Christ—even with all that mess to clean up—God approves of who you are in Him. Christ's righteousness is yours because of what He has already done. Take a minute to look up these verses. And tell God how you feel about His forgiveness.

Psalm 103:8-18 • Romans 5:6-11 • Hebrews 12:18-24

BLAİSE PASCAL

"This is eternal life: that they may know You, the only true God, and the One You have sent—Jesus Christ."

—John 17:3

BLAISE PASCAL
FIRE!

PARIS, FRANCE · 1654

Sometimes personal tastes and preferences become matters of self-righteous pride, and we belittle the value and opinions of others who simply have a different bent than we do. If someone happens to be a bit too intellectual for our blood, we tend to consider their obsession with theories and abstractions a bunch of baloney, an almost sinful waste of time. Real people who need real things continue to suffer for a lack of real Christian love. And all the thinkers want to do is argue their pet points of doctrine.

Meanwhile, the lovers of ideas often look down their noses at the common men who breezily insist that the answers to life's complexities are as simple as "praying about it," who think that no amount of study is really required to become like Christ, that the truest form of Christian living is always the practical, with little thought given to the beliefs that drive the practice.

Intellectual prejudice truly runs both ways.

But in Blaise Pascal, both the uneducated and the egghead find a friend, a man who confidently held the hand of logic yet reached across the cultural spectrum to grasp the shoulder of the simple follower of Christ, bringing both of them together in a beautiful picture of God's diversely unified Body.

For Pascal was a man who lived and thrived in the rarefied air of science and speculation. At a startlingly young age, he was already amazing the doctored and degreed with his unusual understanding of geometry, mathematics, fluid mechanics.

This guy was good. Any 16-year-old who could write a detailed treatise on the sections of a cone was certainly worth his ice cream.

He invented the first calculating machine, the first syringe, the first hydraulic lift. He discovered and proved the theory that air pressure changes at various altitudes, and then *dis*proved the accepted view that "nature abhors a vacuum" by creating one himself with a flask of mercury. He even conceived and created the first public transportation system as a way of alleviating the sufferings of the peasant class. He was a man of letters, motivated by a heart of love.

But even though he spent many sleepless hours in lofty regions of thought to which few of us ever even find the ladder, he fully understood that there was a limit to pondering the unproveable.

"The heart has its reasons, which reason does not know. It is the heart which experiences God, and not the reason."

Yes, people of faith need to think. But thinkers need to be people of faith.

"Jesus Christ is the object of all things, the center upon which all things focus. Whoever knows Him knows the reason for everything."

And fire!

Despite all the words that filled the rooms in his exalted vocabulary, this was the only one that could come close to describing what happened to him the night of November 23, 1654. "From about half past ten at night to about half an hour after midnight. . . .

"Fire!"

The blaze had been lit years before. And it had been burning slowly ever since. In 1651 Pascal's father had dislocated his thigh in a fall. Through the influence of two men who came into their home to care for him, Pascal's entire family had been converted to Christ. But the prideful pull of philosophy had been too great. He soon found himself much more in love with learning—and with its heady, egotistical enjoyment—than with anything born of his newfound faith. Had it not been for a late October accident, when his horses had snapped their reins and hurtled over a bridge to their deaths in the River Seine, leaving Pascal safe but askew in the overturned carriage, he might have been willing to put up with the annoying heat of God's Spirit inside him the rest of his life.

"Without Scripture, whose only object is to proclaim Christ, we know nothing, and we can see nothing but obscurity and confusion in the nature of God and in nature itself."

But with his Bible open to John 17:3 that November night—with the shock of near death drawing his attention toward eternal life—the heat became a roaring inferno, the pillars of reason began to shake and smolder, and the knowledge of God exploded throughout a mind accustomed to great insights and revelations . . . but nothing like this!

"This is eternal life: that they may *know* You, the only true God, and the One You have sent—Jesus Christ."

Pascal's words shot out in quick bursts of ecstasy.

"Joy, joy, tears of joy. . . . The world forgotten, everything except God. . . . I am separated from Him, for I have shunned Him, denied Him, crucified Him. . . . Let me not be cut off from Him forever."

Suddenly the Scriptures he had studied in the past began raining through the flames. "My God and your God" (John 20:17). "Your God shall be my God" (Ruth 1:16). "Righteous Father, the world has not known You, but I have known You" (John 17:25). "I will not neglect Your Word" (Psalm 119:16).

In two holy hours of trembling conviction, bordering on terror yet washed with the tears of repentance, he found "certitude, heartfelt joy, peace . . . complete and sweet renunciation . . . total submission to Jesus Christ . . . everlasting joy in return for one day's striving."

The fire had caught.

He had seen the utter despair of his hopeless condition. "For we desire truth and find ourselves with nothing but uncertainty. We seek happiness and find only misery and death." Even in the Incarnation of Christ, he saw the dire straits of human sin "through the greatness of the remedy it requires."

But because of this glorious "remedy," Pascal had tasted the boundless love of God. He had tasted the mercy God showers on the human soul. He had fallen facedown on the ground, giving glory to God for providing him something he could never discover on his own—a way to worship Him, to commune with Him.

To know Him.

"Not only do we know God only through Jesus Christ, but we know ourselves only through Jesus Christ. Apart from Jesus Christ we cannot know the meaning of our life or of our death, of God or of ourselves."

Only one thing is really worth knowing. And He is our Redeemer.

Pascal never forgot his fiery experience with God. He even sewed the piece of parchment containing his memories of that night into his clothing and carried it with him at all times.

And when he redesigned his coat of arms two years later, he underlined it with the words of 2 Timothy 1:12: "I know whom I have believed."

In other words, *I don't just "think, therefore I am."*
I believe.
Therefore I know.

WHAT'S YOUR STORY?

"God has placed the parts, each one of them, in the body just as He want-
ed"—for each to do its part, to invest time and perform tasks that complete
the work of the church without competing against each other. Have you been
able to get comfortable letting people be who God has made them to be with-
out insisting they be more like you? And have you gained the courage to do
what you know God has called you to do whether others appreciate it or not?

Matthew 18:1-4 • Romans 12:3-13 • Galatians 6:3-5

PATRICK
OF IRELAND

"When they hand you over, don't worry
about how or what you should speak.
For you will be given what to say at
that hour, because you are not speaking,
but the Spirit of your Father is speaking
in you."

—Matthew 10:19-20

PATRICK
OF IRELAND
SPIRITUALLY SPEAKING

THE COAST OF BRITAIN · 430

Most historians admit to being a little ignorant about the exact details of Patrick's life.

That's okay. Patrick admitted to being a little ignorant himself.

"I am Patrick, a sinner, most uncultivated and the least of all the faithful . . . very little educated . . . like a stone that lies in deep mud."

He wasn't being falsely humble. He was simply stating the facts.

Yet he did have a good excuse for missing out on whatever educational opportunities existed for a young man of means in early fifth-century Britain. Saxon pirates had raided his father's seaside estate when Patrick was only 16 and carried him off to Ireland, where he tended sheep for the next six years. So while some of his contemporaries were crossing over to the Continent to bathe in language and literature, Patrick was busy leading his herds to high pasture and scratching the ticks off his ankles. While many were passing him hopelessly by in the fields of intellectual pursuits, *his* fields were only for grazing and sleeping and the boredom of lost boyhood.

And though he sometimes wished his early life had been devoted to a sheepskin instead of the sheep pen, he never tried to fake what he hadn't earned outright. "I cannot hold forth in speech to cultivated people in exact language, expressing what my spirit and mind desire and my heart's sentiment indicates. . . . I long in my old age for that which I did not achieve as a youth."

So from the few things we know about Patrick's life, we can accurately conclude that he must have been a wonderful guy, a faithful follower of Christ, a tender and trusting soul.

But he was no whiz in the classroom.

For God had not called him to scholarly pursuits but to prayer—"as many as a hundred prayers in one day, and nearly as many at night, even when I was staying out in the woods or on the mountain. I used to rise before dawn for prayer, in snow and frost and rain, and I used to feel no ill effect, and there was no slackness in me . . . because the Spirit was glowing in me."

Even as a helpless captive in a foreign country, God had been filling him with a power more potent than books and knowledge, a skill more exacting than grammar and syntax, a confidence that drank from a well deeper than ego and the Greek classics.

The Spirit was glowing inside him. And all Ireland would one day feel the fire.

But not yet. Yes, it was in Ireland where his heart had finally been drawn near to God. It was here—on her moors and marshlands, amid her sweetbriers and shamrocks—that he had first approached his Lord out of something other than formal obligation.

"I am a slave of Christ in an outlandish nation, because of the unspeakable glory of eternal life which is in Christ Jesus our Lord."

But when he wasn't thinking of Christ, he was thinking of escape.

Asleep one night on the hillside, he heard a voice in a dream, telling him he would soon return to his homeland. Not too many nights later, his dreams unearthed more specific instructions: "Look, your ship is ready." And though the sea was a good 200 miles away, Patrick decided to brave the danger, to slip away from his captors and into the Irish countryside, heading for the coastland and the unfurled sail that would steer him back to British soil.

After only three days of sea travel the boat made landfall, but the barrier of the Cambrian Mountains and the entire expanse of the nation lay between him and home on the opposite coast. Food became scarce, and his intemperate traveling companions began boiling over in his direction.

"What now, Christian? You say that your God is great and almighty. Why then can you not pray for us? We are in danger of starvation!"

Patrick winced. He looked cowardly into their desperate eyes. Running into the hills began looking like a good option. Instead he found these courageous words forming on his lips:

"Turn in faith with all your heart to the Lord my God, because nothing is impossible to Him. He may today send food across your way until you are full, because He has abundant resources everywhere."

For a moment, silence. A gentle stirring of the wind, a bird's song lilting above the stillness. Then a rustling, rooting noise started up from the thick tangle of brush and vines rimming their footpath, and a herd of pigs tramped stupidly into clear view as if ordered off the menu.

Naturally, the men's hateful threats vanished into hearty cheers. But

> "I daily expect either assassination, trickery, or slavery, but I fear none of these things, because I have thrown myself into the hands of Almighty God."

Patrick knew there was nothing natural about this turn of events. Something *super*natural had occurred that afternoon.

And if he didn't know it then, he would definitely know it before the next morning.

For in the deep watches of that very night, Patrick tossed and turned under the weight of a vicious nightmare. In his dream, "something like a huge stone" fell heavily across his body, rendering his arms and legs incapable of moving. He cried out to God, gasping for breath, straining without success to recover the use of his pinned limbs. Then out of nowhere the sun appeared, rising in the sky, its warm rays inching across his frame, instantly relieving his paralysis and restoring his strength.

As he awoke from the dream, he knew at once that the sun's rays which had released his immovable burden were a picture of "Christ my Lord. His Spirit was at that moment crying out on my behalf . . . as it says in the gospel, 'In that day,' the Lord testifies, 'it will not be you who will speak but the Spirit of your Father who speaks in you.' "

And from that moment on, he knew that following Christ would not require a university degree. Instead it would actually require something much harder to achieve—a submissive faith which understood that "He who gave His life for you, He it is who speaks in you."

So when the visionary call came to Patrick to "come and walk among us again"—to return to the land of his captivity and preach the gospel to the lost souls in Ireland—he responded to such strange logic with the oddity of total obedience.

And oh, how they came to the light he proclaimed! How they marvelled at such compelling words flowing from such ordinary lips. Many thousands, in fact, were swept into the Kingdom on the wings of Patrick's message. And when men of the church—men of letters—hustled over from Britain to protest the work of this unschooled, self-styled bishop, "violently pushing to make me fall . . . the Lord kindly spared His stranger and sojourner for the sake of His name, and greatly supported me when I was downtrodden. How amazing that I did not come to a bad end in failure and disgrace."

Yes, it is amazing, isn't it?

Or perhaps the more amazing fact is that we too often impress ourselves with our own abilities—or too often defeat ourselves with our own inadequacies—and view God's power as either an unnecessary bother or a last resort.

Patrick knew it wasn't about him, but about Who was with him.

"Whoever shall condescend to peruse or to receive this writing which Patrick, a very badly educated sinner, has written in Ireland, nobody shall ever say that it was I, the ignoramus, if I have shown any small success according to God's pleasure, but you are to think and it must be sincerely believed that it was the gift of God. And this is my Confession before I die."

Doesn't sound so stupid after all.

WHAT'S YOUR STORY?

You may not recognize it when it happens. In fact, God may choose never to reveal to you the impact your words and actions had on someone else's life. But it isn't about you anyway. It's all about Him. Is your devotion deep enough, your love pure enough, your motivation unselfish enough that you can remain obedient to God even when the credit never comes your way?

Exodus 4:10-12 • Jeremiah 1:4-9 • John 3:25-30

PAUL ✝HE APOS✝LE

"I will also appoint you as a light for the nations, to be My salvation to the ends of the earth."

—*Isaiah 49:6*

PAUL THE APOSTLE
TO THE NATIONS

DAMASCUS, SYRIA · 35

Having his life story recorded so familiarly in the Bible shouldn't disqualify Paul from being included among Christian history's greatest heroes. Just because his biography has come down to us in chapters and verses and Sunday School lessons doesn't place his monumental life in some alternate, spiritual universe—detached from everything else that was really going on in the first-century world.

And just because he wrote nearly half the books of the New Testament shouldn't make it impossible that he too could have a favorite verse—a Word from God that motivated him to "pursue the prize" of "God's heavenly call," even when it meant beatings and stonings and months of prison time . . . or a cold, sharp axe to the back of the neck, which probably came his way somewhere around 64 A.D.

For most of us, the calling of God has come with its share of mystery. We've wondered at times what God was saying about His will for our lives. Was it really Him? Was it maybe us—what we were wanting Him to be saying?

Paul's calling, on the other hand—(as you know)—arrived like a 2 x 4 across the bridge of the nose. Throbbing light, cranked to a piercing frequency, knocking him to his knees, blinding all sight from his open eyes. *Hello. This is God. Do I have your attention?*

Uh, yes.

God's orders were these: Take the message of His love and salvation beyond the strict borders of Judaism, to the heathens and pagans who in God's timing were about to come into an inheritance they never knew existed!

Paul couldn't deny what God was saying. Yet he could hardly believe what he was hearing.

Paul had been born a Jew in a foreign land. Generations earlier, his family had apparently relocated from Palestine (directly or indirectly) to the city of Tarsus, which remains to this day—as it was then—a bustling city a few miles inland on Turkey's southern shore.

His Jewish name, of course, was Saul. Maybe he was named after his grandfather or another respected relative, or maybe after the first king of Israel—himself a fellow member and historical giant from the tribe of Benjamin. But whatever the roots of his Jewish name, Paul's roots had been planted firmly in the Jewish tradition from an early age . . . as a Pharisee, a "separated one," like his father. He likely learned to read and write by copying passages from the Scriptures, being immersed by his teachers in the ancient Hebrew language and the sacred texts we now call the Old Testament, eventually spending his youth under the instruction of a well-known rabbi in Jerusalem.

The Jewish heritage was his bread and butter. And he intended to spend his life defending it from those who threatened to dilute or dismantle it—primarily those who claimed to be followers of that blasphemous upstart from Nazareth . . . the man named Jesus.

In fact, rooting out the Christians was what he was on his way to do the

"God wanted to make known to those among the Gentiles the glorious wealth of this mystery, which is Christ in you, the hope of glory."

day God brought up the lights along the road from Jerusalem to Damascus, as the voice of the risen Christ spoke to him from the heavens: "Saul, Saul . . . I am Jesus, whom you are persecuting."

As the days unfolded, God continued defining the mission: Paul was to be His "chosen instrument to carry My name before Gentiles, kings, and the sons of Israel." Like anyone who's been persuaded to question the particular culture and mindset they were brought up in, Paul must have wracked his brain to see how this could square with all the things he'd been taught, the observations he had made, the Scriptures he had read.

But with the scales lifted from his eyes, suddenly the Scriptures he revered seemed full of this new revelation:

"I live by faith in the Son of God, who loved me and gave Himself for me. I do not set aside the grace of God; for if righteousness comes through the law, then Christ died for nothing."

• "This is why the promise is by faith, so that it may be according to grace, to guarantee it to all the descendants—not only to those who are of the law, but also to those who are of Abraham's faith. He is the father of us all in God's sight. As it is written: 'I have made you the father of many nations.'"

• "As He also says in Hosea, 'I will call "Not-My-People," "My-People," and she who is "Unloved," "Beloved." And it will be in the place where they were told, you are not My people, there they will be called sons of the living God.'"

• "And Isaiah says boldly, 'I was found by those who were not looking for Me; I revealed Myself to those who were not asking for Me. . . . Those who had no report of Him will see, and those who have not heard will understand.' "

But of all the passages that now rang through his mind with this liberating, global appeal, none was more real and personal than this one: "I will also appoint you as a light for the nations, to be My salvation to the ends of the earth."

When he and his companions would venture into a city and begin freely sharing Christ's glorious gospel to those who had never heard such things, the Jewish establishment would rush in to stop the hemorrhaging—the loss of control, the winds of change, the distortion of truth. Their outrage would invariably escalate into slander and violence. Paul would be dragged before the authorities, accused of causing a disturbance, and run out of town . . . if not whipped within an inch of his life to make it official.

Yet Paul would turn to his accusers and boldly declare, "It was necessary that God's message be spoken to you first. But since you reject it, and consider yourselves unworthy of eternal life, we now turn to the Gentiles! For this is what the Lord has commanded us: 'I have appointed you as a light for the Gentiles, to bring salvation to the ends of the earth.' "

Again and again, in nearly all of his 13 letters, he would echo this driving refrain. Yes, he was proud of his Jewish upbringing. His love for his fellow Hebrews never wavered in the face of their hostile persecutions. The Greeks and Romans knew how to pour it on, too, responding to his attacks on their immoral, idolatrous lifestyles by slapping him in jail or leaving him twisting in the wind in the face of a riotous mob.

Still, he stayed true to his calling.

Who knows how many times he had to deal with his own flashbacks— memories of the terror he had enjoyed raining on Christ's followers, the faces of those he had stoned into martyrdom, the shrieks of their wives and children begging hysterically for mercy.

Still, he stayed true to his calling.

Many who had once stood beside him deserted him along the way. But just before his date with a Roman executioner, he wrote in his final letter that "the Lord stood with me and strengthened me, so that the proclamation might be fully made through me, and all the Gentiles might hear." Paul had "fought the good fight . . . finished the race . . . kept the faith."

He had stayed true to his calling—his calling to the nations.

WHAT'S YOUR STORY?

There is not a stranger you'll meet today who is unworthy to hear the Good News of God's salvation. There is not a husband, or uncle, or neighbor, or coworker, or movie star (for that matter) who is beyond hope of having God spin them around in the road and make His loving plans for them crystal clear. Keep praying, keep proclaiming, keep persevering. This Word is for everyone.

Isaiah 60:1-3 • Acts 2:37-40 • Romans 10:5-13

WILLIAM
PENN

Whatever has been born of God conquers the world. This is the victory that has conquered the world: our faith.

—1 John 5:4

WILLIAM PENN
MAN WITH A PLAN

CORK, IRELAND · 1666

His father, Admiral Sir William Penn, was a decorated naval officer, a man of war, a friend of kings. He fought for honor, duty, and country.

But the son of the great sailor, the boy William Penn, would grow up quietly around the house, playing games, minding his schoolwork. And preparing to fight for God.

By his thirties, young William Penn would become perhaps the leading defender of religious tolerance in all of England. He would use his family connections to spring hundreds of Christians from the jailhouse—and save scores of others from the gallows. Yet before his many scrapes with the British authorities were over, he would land in prison six times himself, even hide in the squalid London slums for four years as a fugitive.

And his military, spit-and-polish father would say out loud that he wished his disgraceful son had never been born.

But William Penn saw the world differently from his father. And he would conquer it in his own way—in a different way.

By faith.

Wasn't that what the traveling preacher said that day? Thomas Loe had been holding a meeting in the southern Ireland town where William was managing his father's estate. William had heard him speak twice before— once as a child, once as a student at Oxford. And each time he had been captured by his humble magnetism, his uncommon blend of soft-spoken simplicity and undaunted courage.

Yet there was something about this third encounter with the old Quaker preacher that penetrated a deep place in William Penn's soul. Something about that verse. Something about faith being the victory, faith overcoming the world.

Think of it: If William's whole world had revolved around himself, then a life of effortless ease was within his grasp. There were his daddy's personal affairs to manage, or a law education to practice, or just about anything he desired from his cordial relationship with King Charles II and the king's brother, the duke of York—soon to be King James II.

"No pain, no palm; no thorns, no throne; no gall, no glory; no cross, no crown. . . . We cannot love to live, if we cannot bear to die."

But God was beginning to open William's mind to a much larger world— a New World—where victory was far from assured, and faith in God would be the only connection he could count on.

It didn't take him long to start needing it.

September 1667. Police break into a Quaker meeting—a group of Protestants more officially called the Society of Friends. Their demeanor (as always) is quiet, solemn, passive, yet perceived as a threat to the state-run church. William, out of place in his aristocratic fashions among the plain dress and simple manners of these unpretentious folk, is freed, released, apologized to. But unwilling to distance himself from his newly found Christian brothers, he refuses. *He was now one of them*, he said, *and he wanted to be treated so.*

Before long it would be the Anglican bishop himself who would demand

William's arrest, clapping him in the notorious Tower of London for speaking his mind on religious matters in defiance of the high church. Ordered to recant, William sealed a seven-month sentence by declaring, "My prison shall be my grave before I will budge a jot, for I owe my conscience to no mortal man."

In and out of prison. Arguing his own defense in the courts. Traveling to other persecuted regions and lifting the spirits of the oppressed. For twelve years or more, he lived on the edge with his convictions, until he slowly began to realize that his fight was futile. England would never stop coercing its citizens to conform to the crown's religion, would never stop cramming its will down the throats of the people.

A weaker man might have just stood by and watched his vision sink. But defeated on one shore, William Penn decided to run up the sail and conquer another one.

"Love is the hardest lesson in Christianity; but, for that reason, it should be most of our care to learn it. Those things are most difficult which are most beautiful."

He made arrangements to appear before his royal acquaintances with a proposal—acquiring a piece of pioneering land an ocean away where he could establish an American colony. In return, he'd forget a £16,000 debt the state owed to his deceased father's estate. *And besides, what better way to get rid of those pesky Quakers for good—huh, King?*

The bait worked.

On November 8, 1682, he stepped foot on the west bank of the Delaware River, into a land the king desired to name "The Forests of Penn"—not in honor of the William Penn who cut the deal, but his late father, the great Admiral William Penn of England.

Pennsylvania. An appeal to the son's loyalty.

But to William, it was his "holy experiment." A world to conquer by faith.

Nearly a hundred years before the signing of the Declaration of Independence, he brought the first vestige of government to this ragtag band of German and Dutch settlers and created a haven for thousands more who were fleeing persecution in their homelands—a place where "no one can be put out of his estate and subjected to the political view of another, without his consent." Even in some of the surrounding colonies, Quakers were being whipped, tarred, and hanged as heretics. But in Pennsylvania, William provided all peace-loving people a sanctuary of freedom.

Were it not for the Indians.

Squabbles and skirmishes with the Native Americans had created a nervous horror throughout almost all the colonies. Certainly, both sides had given as good as they had gotten. One night a colonial settlement might be raided and ransacked; the next, an Indian village would be burned, its inhabitants massacred. The threat loomed everywhere—in the treetops, the morning fog, the thickets that camouflaged attack.

But William determined to conquer even this world—not with fire or stealth or ambush—but by faith. Always by faith.

That's why he learned the languages of the native tribes. That's why he strode into their encampments without guards or guns at his side. That's why he participated in their contests, ate their foods, sought their good, and enjoyed their company.

One day, as history tells us, William and his Indian friends gathered under the great elm at Shakamaxon and agreed that they would live in peace. No papers were signed, no demands were pressed, no blood was spilled. But in shaking hands they shook the world. Their accord prevailed beyond his life-time, and not one Quaker was known to have been killed by the neighboring tribes.

His faith had won the victory—over prejudice, over tyranny, over war.

His faith in God had conquered a world.

WHAT'S YOUR STORY?

What plans and dreams has God given you, only to see them languishing as scrap pieces of paper and weekend promises? Don't expect the path to be lined with runway lights, with every question answered and every space colored in. The discovery of God's will is an exercise in faith, not a reliance on facts and figures. Hear it from some people who've been there . . .

Exodus 3:1-15 • 2 Chronicles 20:1-17 • Hebrews 11:29-34

CHARLES
SPURGEON

"Turn to Me and be saved, all the ends of the earth, for I am God, and there is no other."

—Isaiah 45:22

CHARLES SPURGEON
LOOK HERE, YOUNG MAN

COLCHESTER, ENGLAND · 1850

It was one of those snowstorms that nearly blinded your vision, stinging you in the face and sneaking under your coat collar. And even though Charles Spurgeon was all for going to church that Sunday morning, he was also just 15-years-old. And more than willing to settle for the first place he came to.

So after ducking down a side street to shield himself from the bitter wind, he found himself stamping the snow from his boots, not in his father's church but in a Primitive Methodist Chapel on Artillery Street.

He and about 15 other people.

The fill-in preacher was terrible. For ten minutes or so, the man wrestled to gather a complete thought, twisting his way through endless loops of logic and fighting a losing battle with the English language. But swiftly reaching the end of his ideas, the preacher noticed the teenaged visitor sitting alone under the balcony . . . and suddenly located the inspiration he had been looking for.

"Young man, you're in trouble!"—his thin, trembling voice treading higher —his bony pointer finger gunning in Spurgeon's direction. "The Lord says, 'Look unto me, and be ye saved, all the ends of the earth.' Look to Jesus Christ!

"Look! Look! Look!"

The warmth of the stove had just begun to reach Spurgeon's cold hands and feet, but now the warmth of God's Word had reached the cold, needy corners of his heart, "and in that moment I saw the sun! Oh, I did look! I could almost have looked my eyes away! . . . I saw what a Savior Christ was. I believed in one moment!

"And as the snow fell on my road home from that little house of prayer, I thought every snowflake talked with me and told me of the pardon I had found, for I was as white as the driven snow through the grace of God."

Charles Spurgeon was utterly converted. That day. By that verse.

And throughout his life, he never forgot it. Granted, his printed sermons number into the thousands—enough to fill a standard encyclopedia set—but in nearly 300 of his messages he returned to the little chapel on Artillery Street, to the little preacher who locked eyes on the back wall of Spurgeon's soul, and who brought to his knees the man who would one day bring all London to its feet.

Within the next five years, Spurgeon would complete his basic schooling (which was all the formal education he ever received), fill a small pulpit in the hamlet of Waterbeach, then be called to the 300-member New Park Street Chapel in London as its permanent pastor.

He was 19 years old.

By June of the next year, despite an expanded sanctuary that seated close to 1,500 people, more than 3,000 were coming every Sunday—morning and evening—practically sitting in each other's laps in order

"Get a view of Christ and you have seen more than mountains and cascades and valleys and seas. Earth may give its beauty, but all these put together can never rival Him."

to hear this baby-faced preaching machine. Yet the crowds kept growing. By October 1856 the church had leased Surrey Music Hall for their Sunday services, the largest public arena in all of London. As many as 12,000 filled the auditorium for the first morning worship there—with 10,000 others milling at the doors and in the streets. But the program had hardly begun before someone mysteriously yelled "Fire!" from one of the balconies. Waves of panic rippled through the worshipers, and huge numbers were injured in the pandemonium. Seven were killed.

Spurgeon was inconsolable.

In only two years he had risen from total obscurity to become not only a darling national figure but a known leader on the world stage. Now, however, he found himself the subject of bitter editorials, a caricature in newspaper cartoons, and—hardest to take—a lightning rod for criticism from other Christian ministers. The cumulative weight of his church's tragedy and these personal attacks took their treacherous toll, and Spurgeon sank into a deep, dark depression.

> "It is blessed to eat into the very soul of the Bible until, at last, you come to talk in scriptural language, and your spirit is flavored with the words of the Lord."

In fact, he never really came out of it the rest of his life.

At any place, at any time, the dreadful scene from that fatal day could take a detour through his conscious thoughts, and he would feel himself being beaten to the ground, unable to move, to respond, to function. "The chariot wheels drag heavily. Even prayer seems like labor. Yes, the chariot wheels drag heavily, yet they are not taken off."

You'd have had a hard time spotting it in him, though. For the next 31 years he led his church with bold eloquence and visionary leadership. He founded more then 60 organizations and wrote more than 140 books. He often worked 18 hours a day, giving a full afternoon each week to nothing other than one-on-one, face-to-face, personal ministry and evangelism. There is no telling how many people—or how many generations—felt the after-shocks of his faithful witness.

But among the other physical ailments that dogged his steps and shortened his life, the leaden spectre of depression never let go, never let up, never let on.

Or did it?

"I am afraid that all the grace that I have gotten from my comfortable and easy times might almost lie on a penny. But the good that I have received from my sorrows and pains and griefs is altogether incalculable. Affliction is the best bit of furniture in my house. It is the best book in a minister's library."

For he saw his depression for what it was—a strange gift from God, a way to understand the heavy burdens carried by so many in this world, a trigger that alerted his mind to a deeper phase of spiritual dependence. "Depression has now become to me as a prophet in rough clothing, a John the Baptist heralding the nearer coming of my Lord's richer blessing. . . . I would go into the deeps a hundred times to cheer a downcast spirit. It is good for me to have been afflicted, that I might know how to speak a word in season to one that is weary."

Often as he delivered his sermons, "I heard my own chains clank while I tried to preach to my fellow prisoners in the dark." He would freely tell his congregation, "I am feeling low." And in that admission, his hearers would find the strength to join him in looking up, in looking to Jesus, in looking beyond their problems to the One whose very presence could burn a shaft of purpose into any earthly hardship.

"The word that drew my soul—'Look unto me'—still rings its clarion note in my ears. There I once found conversion, and there I shall ever find renewal."

The day of his funeral—at age 57—more than 60,000 onlookers gazed upon his casket, where a Bible lay open to Isaiah 45:22: "Look unto me all ye ends of the earth." For he had seen his glorious Savior as a boy, had pointed thousands upon thousands to Him as a man, and now gazed upon Him in glory with his very own eyes.

Just one look. That's all it took.

WHAT'S YOUR STORY?

Where have you been looking—when your house won't sell, when your children won't mind, when your money won't stretch, when your coworkers won't cooperate? Yes, one look to Jesus will save your soul, but it takes a steady stare into His loving face to keep the rest of your life in perspective, to keep trust from deteriorating into trauma, to keep the everyday from clouding the everlasting. Look to Jesus today, and promise you'll never look back.

Philippians 3:17-21 • Hebrews 12:1-3 • 1 John 1:1-4

HUDSON
TAYLOR

"I am the vine; you are the branches. The one who remains in Me and I in him produces much fruit, because you can do nothing without Me."

—John 15:5

HUDSON TAYLOR
IN HIS GRIP

CHIN-KIANG, CHINA · 1869

With the kind of lofty dreams and goals God had given to Hudson Taylor, he knew beyond a shadow of a doubt that "if we are to be much used of Him, we must live very near to Him." He had said so himself. He had *lived* so himself. Anyone looking in from the outside would testify that Hudson Taylor lived about as near to God as a man possibly could.

When the doors had opened for him at age 21 to leave behind his British homeland and sail to China as a Christian missionary, he had willingly pushed the pause button on his medical training at London Hospital and climbed aboard a clipper on his way to Shanghai. He had heard from God.

But the next six years were tough—not just the homesickness, or the unpredictable tasks of pioneering work, or the rude adjustments to a new culture and climate. Those would have all been challenge enough, but—truth be told—even the other missionaries had started to bug him. They seemed soft, comfortable, more eager to be liked than to be daring.

See, China in 1853 was only open to foreigners as far as the trading ports. Sure, there were plenty of prospects for Christ in those cities—and missionaries who were already on the ground to bring the gospel to them. But what about inland? What about the 200 million or more who lived along the rivers and canals that snaked back into the continent—people who worked the land every day and washed their clothes at the water's edge without a clue that Jesus had died, that Jesus had risen, that Jesus Christ was the Son of God?

Taylor and a few brave others had dared on several occasions to venture into the forbidden backlands. He had seen the hunger—and the hatred. His preaching had been received kindly at times, cruelly at others. He had opened his medical bag to the sick, yet also exposed his life to thrown rocks and thievery.

When sickness sent him packing for home in 1860, he left with much work undone, with plans still in the imagination stage, not knowing if he'd ever be back.

"It is not in what He is to me, not in what He is working, or has worked, or may work in me, but in Himself that I am to rejoice."

But even from afar, he stayed near. Near to God. Near enough to keep working on a revision of the New Testament in colloquial Chinese. Near enough to complete the medical degree he knew could become one of his greatest inroads to the inland. Near enough to stand on the shores of Brighton along the English Channel and ask God for 24 new missionaries to take with him to the unreached provinces of China.

It was an audacious prayer. Because if anything, China was closing to Christian influence. The total missionary population had dwindled to under a hundred. Finding two dozen people willing to go at a time when most of the missionaries who were already there were unwilling to stay was almost laughable. Doing it with no money, no organization, and a bold inland vision that no one had ever attempted before was where the joke quit being even funny.

"But if we are obeying the Lord," Taylor said, "the responsibility rests with Him, not with us! Thou, Lord, shalt have all the burden! At thy bidding I go forward, leaving the results with thee."

So for one of the first times in his life, Taylor quit clinging so hard to stay near to God. And realized in letting go that God was actually the One who was clinging hard to him.

The mission was on, but the load was off.

Peace comes hard, however, for driven men like Hudson Taylor—the kind of peace that could let him go to bed on time when his mind was still alive with things to do and letters to write. The kind of peace that could think of no more productive way to spend an hour than in prayer and Bible reading. The kind of peace that could stare into an empty wallet and see a nice opening for the promises of God.

Taylor knew a peace like that from time to time. When people began to respond to his appeal for the "million a month" who were dying without the gospel in China, he would simply say that "the Lord caused them to be interested." When the funds necessary for such an ambitious enterprise were slow in springing up, he would remind those around him that "although the wants are large, they will not exhaust the resources of our Father. There are plenty of ravens in China, and the Lord could send them again with bread and flesh."

"God's work done in God's way will never lack for God's supplies."

So one year after releasing his

> "Jesus is our strength; and what we cannot do or bear, He can both do and bear in us. We are not our own, nor is the work ours. He whose we are and whom we serve will not prove unequal to the emergency."

burden into the hands of God, Taylor, his wife and children, and the 24 new missionaries he had let God be responsible for were on their way to China.

The work—as expected—was endless and demanding. For the most part, his band of pioneers were devoted to the cause and devoid of selfish intentions, yet squabbles inevitably cropped up that took his time away from nobler duties. Taylor's insistence that every member of the China Inland Mission adopt the dress and hairstyles of the native people chafed the Western dignities of a difficult few. And rumors even began floating from disgruntled workers to homeland donors that Taylor was a bit too friendly with the single women in the group.

It was enough to make a man go back to fighting—a time when the spirit can forget what the mind knows, that God was the One who had him here, and God was the One who would keep him near.

It took a letter from a friend—and a special verse of Scripture—to bring that truth back home to a tiring Hudson Taylor. The letter reminded him of the importance of "abiding, not striving nor struggling, but looking off unto Him, resting in the love of an almighty Savior."

Taylor got the message: "As I read, I saw it all! I looked to Jesus and saw (and when I saw, oh, how joy flowed!) that He had said, 'I will never leave you.' Ah, there is rest! I have striven in vain to rest in Him. I'll strive no more. For has He not promised to abide with me—never to leave me, never to fail me?

"As I thought of the Vine and the branches, what light the blessed Spirit poured direct into my soul! I saw not only that Jesus would never leave me, but that I was a member of His body, of His flesh, and of His bones. The vine (now I see) is not the root merely, but all—root, stem, branches, twigs, leaves, flowers, fruit. And Jesus is not only that: He is soil and sunshine, air and showers, and ten thousand times more than we have ever dreamed, wished for, or needed. Oh, the joy of seeing this truth! . . . I have seen it long enough in the Bible, but I *believe* it now as a living reality.

"I have not got to *make* myself a branch. The Lord Jesus tells me I *am* a branch!"

For years he had labored to be faithful in his devotions, faultless in his conduct, fearless in his circumstances. He had pushed himself beyond strength, straining to stay near to God, near to His Word, near to His guidance. But now he understood afresh—the branch doesn't fight to stay attached to the Vine. The strength of the Vine is what holds the branch in place.

"So if God should place me in great perplexity, must He not give me much guidance; in positions of great difficulty, much grace; in circumstances of great pressure and trial, much strength? I have no fear that His resources will be unequal to the emergency! His resources are mine, for He is mine, He is with me, and He dwells in me."

"I am a new man," he told his closest friends. A man at peace. A man whose China Inland Mission would grow into hundreds of workers reaching hundreds of thousands for Christ, establishing an unprecedented Christian presence in every province of China.

But only because the Vine had opened a new branch there.

WHAT'S YOUR STORY?

If you've grown tired of trusting God to use your life for a real and meaningful purpose, immerse yourself in the truth that He will accomplish His work through you—in His way, at His time, for His glory. Spending time with God will cease to be a constant chore and duty when you have submitted your way to Him and found His strength to be all you really need.

Psalm 62:5-12 • Hosea 14:1-9 • 2 Corinthians 12:7-10

CORRIE
TEN BOOM

Because you have limited strength, have kept My word, and have not denied My name, look, I have placed before you an open door that no one is able to close.

—Revelation 3:8

CORRIE
TEN BOOM
THE OPEN DOOR POLICY

RAVENSBRUCK, GERMANY · 1944

"Corrie, we are in hell."

For three stifling days and nights, the endless row of closed boxcars had lurched, yanked, and jerked its human freight across the Dutch border and deep into Nazi Germany, finally dumping its load onto the wretched outskirts of death and indignity.

The Ravensbruck Extermination Camp, fifty miles north of Berlin in Hitler's Germany. Corrie ten Boom's sister, Betsie, had described it well. They were about as close to hell as a person could get and still call herself alive.

As the throng of bone-weary women stumbled down the hill of hard earth toward an uncertain date with certain death, all was raw fear. Visible horror. Rank disbelief.

But lost among the sounds of shuffling boots and heaving lungs was the muffled thumping of a tiny, unnoticed pouch that hung around Corrie's neck. Inside was the smuggled Bible that had sustained both her and her sister throughout months of torture and imprisonment. Its gentle tapping between thin fabric and shoulder blade seemed to be saying something—asking a bigger question than any of the ones racing through her mind at this hurried moment, at the breathless sight of coiled wire, concrete walls, and sinister smokestacks.

"God's good news. Was it to *this world* that He had spoken it?"

Already she had endured more cruelty and abuse than she had ever thought possible for her role in the Dutch Resistance. First, there had been the raid on their home for harboring Jews—the stinging slaps in the face, the shoves and snatches of interrogating soldiers. Then the long weeks of solitary confinement, the who-cares news of her dear father's death, the lack of food, the rancid conditions, the forced, dehumanizing labor.

Yet even in the midst of such hate and evil, there was always—somehow—God's good news.

> "Faith is like radar that sees through the fog—the reality of things at a distance that the human eye cannot see."

Months earlier a sympathetic nurse had secretly slipped her a small, paper package: two bars of soap, a handful of safety pins, and four little pamphlets: the four Gospels. She gobbled them down, whole books at a time, then haltingly gave them away book by book to others who needed them more—at risk of an even crueler sentence of starvation and punishment. "But that would be a small price to pay, I thought, as I stretched my aching body on the foul straw, for the precious books I clutched between my hands."

On the very day she had placed her last booklet into the hands of a fellow captive—and her need for its company into the hands of God—a surprise visit from her freed sister, Nollie, brought her the compact copy of Scripture that now thudded quietly beneath her prison blouse as she plodded through the iron gates and into the flea-bitten bowels of Ravensbruck.

And indeed, God's news remained good. Even there.

"From morning until lights-out, whenever we were not in ranks for roll call, our Bible was the center of an ever-widening circle of help and hope. Like waifs clustered around a blazing fire, we gathered about it, holding out our hearts to its warmth and light. The blacker the night around us grew, the brighter and truer and more beautiful burned the Word of God.

"Sometimes," she said, "I would slip the Bible from its little sack with hands that shook, so mysterious had it become to me. It was new; it had just been written. I marveled sometimes that the ink was dry. I had believed the Bible always, but reading it now had nothing to do with belief. It was simply a description of the way things were—of how men act and how God acts."

Amid the horrors of holocaust, God's truth was prevailing. And the gates of hell could not resist it.

"When you are dying—when you stand at the gate of eternity—you see things from a different perspective than when you think you may live for a long time. I stood at that gate for many months."

Many died there. Actually, *most* died there. Her sister, Betsie, was one of them. And had Corrie remained in the camp even a few days more—when the order was given to kill all the women her age and older—her story likely would have evaporated with theirs into the thin grey vapor that hung like a pall over the bunks and barracks of Ravensbruck.

But on December 31, 1944, "by a clerical error of man and a miracle of God," Corrie retraced her steps through the heavy, iron gates of holocaust and into the liberating light of release.

It was over.

"Behind me I heard the hinges squeak as the gate swung shut. I was free! And flooding through my mind were the words of Jesus to the church at Philadelphia: 'Behold, I have set before thee an open door, and no man can shut it.' "

By now she was already 52 years old. And the many stressful years of providing refuge for Jewish fugitives plus the ten harsh months of rugged imprisonment had done nothing to encourage her life expectancy.

But she would live the vision that Betsie had received while harnessed in Ravensbruck—"to tell people what we have learned here . . . that there is no pit so deep that He is not deeper still. They will listen to us, Corrie, because we have been here."

By June of the next year, she opened a rehabilitation home she had been given in the Netherlands for the handicapped and the ex-prisoners of concentration camps. She even raised money to purchase a *former* camp in Germany and helped transform it into a haven for those displaced and disabled by the trauma of war. By the time a stroke claimed her ability to speak at age 86, she had traveled and ministered in more than 60 countries around the world.

On the set of *The Hiding Place* in 1975—the motion picture inspired by her family's underground efforts during World War II—Corrie sat and watched the filming of the final scene. The doors of the concentration camp swung open, the actress playing her character joined a handful of others emerging from its vicious hold, and the real-life Corrie sitting quietly behind the cameras, a woman toughened by years of selfless service and unbearable suffering, began to openly weep. Deep sobs. Painful memories. Fury and fear, colliding with faith and forgiveness.

The door was open, yes. But it hurt to see it again from this side, from out here, looking back at all the agony and loss that lay behind it.

Her personal assistant and companion, Ellen, placed an arm around Corrie's shoulder and whispered tearfully into her ear, "God has given you an open door. No one has been able to shut it."

Not even a devil in hell.

WHAT'S YOUR STORY?

Perhaps your past also echoes with the slamming of doors—the loss of your innocence, the death of a dream, the disappointment of unmet expectations. But what if God were to tell you that there are doors in front of you that no one can shut—the door of forgiveness, the door of hope, the door of victory, the door of freedom. What would keep you from walking through them?

Lamentations 3:1-33 • John 8:1-11 • Romans 8:31-39

WILLIAM TYNDALE

We love because He first loved us.

—1 John 4:19

WILLIAM TYNDALE

FIRST LOVE

ANTWERP, BELGIUM · 1531

It's hard for the modern mind to understand why the church of the 1500s was so violently opposed to giving people a Bible they could read.

But light enough martyrs' fires under people just for reciting a favorite passage from memory, or for teaching their children the Ten Commandments, or for having the poor sense to possess a copy in public, and—whether you understand the angry sentiments or not—you can't deny that both church and state were serious about dealing with it. *Dead* serious.

To them the Bible in common, everyday English was a contagion, full of "deadly poison and heresy," good only for "the grievous peril and danger of the souls committed to our charge, and the offense of God's Divine Majesty." Given the choice between living without either God's laws or the pope's commands (as one English clergyman had proposed to William Tyndale one day), they would gladly surrender even their Latin Scriptures and take every one of their spiritual orders from Rome. But Tyndale had a quick response to such disregard for the sacred Word: "I will one day make the boy that drives the plow in England know more of the Scripture than the pope himself!"

Yes, it's hard to understand the paranoia of the priests in the 1500s. Yet it's also hard to understand what could make a promising Cambridge grad like William Tyndale set his plans so squarely in their face, committing himself to the task of translating the Scriptures into English, fully aware that it could easily cost him his life.

Only one explanation is really good enough:

Love.

It was a love he had first discovered while reading the Greek New Testament published by a Dutch scholar named Erasmus. For many centuries up until then, the Bible of record in the West had been the Latin Vulgate, a translation only within reach of the scholar, the privileged, the highly placed. But ransacks and unrest in the East had brought a wave of both new learning and ancient languages blowing into Europe, and this exciting look

"Why should not the sermons of the Apostles, preached no doubt in the mother-tongue of those who heard them, be now written in the mother-tongue of those who read them?"

at the Bible in its original tongue was an invigorating experience for men like Tyndale who were hungry for knowledge. And hungry for God.

He had already learned seven languages. His growing mastery of Greek would soon make it eight. But as he read, what stood out more clearly than the letters on the page was the love of the Father—a love not won by the holy works of grown men, but a love freely given by God to His children before they were even born.

"We love him," the manuscript said, "because he first loved us."

Such love, Tyndale said, was "the pearly gate through which I entered the Kingdom. I used to think that salvation was not for me, since I did not love God, but these precious words showed me that God does not love us because we first loved Him. No, no; we love Him because He first loved us.

"His love makes all the difference!"

> "Christ brings the love of God unto us. He is called in Scripture God's mercy-stool. Whosoever therefore flieth to Christ can neither hear nor receive of God any other thing than mercy."

It made William Tyndale long to see this eternal Word in the leathery hands of the peasant, the weary hands of the milkmaid, the trembling hands of the aged. It made him choose to leave his English homeland—never to return—because "there was no room for attempting a translation of the Scriptures there."

And it made him a wanted man by none other than King Henry VIII, whose minions had spotted Tyndale's work spinning off the printing press in Cologne, Germany, and had rushed in to seize it.

But Tyndale had gotten advance word of their snooping and had beaten them to the print shop, hustling off with as many sheets as he could grab to the nearby city of Worms, where in 1526 he succeeded in printing 6,000 copies of the entire New Testament— the first pure translation of the Greek into English, reproduced not one at a time, handwritten over a period of months, but in a matter of days—by the hundreds. Pretty soon, Tyndale's tiny editions were finding their way across the water into England, tucked inside bales of cloth and sacks of flour.

It was a flood no man could stop. Sure, thousands of copies were discovered by tipped-off authorities at the customs point and were set ablaze in public ceremonies at St. Paul's Cross—a "burnt offering most pleasing to almighty God," the bishop of London had pronounced it.

"But in burning the New Testament, they did nothing other than what I looked for," Tyndale said, for neither the nosy dockworkers nor the lapping flames could keep *every* copy from entering the country—or restrain the love of God that was now brightening hearts every day in the homes and hamlets of Tyndale's people. "No more shall they do if they burn me also, if it be God's will."

They would get around to that.

But finding a lone translator loose somewhere on the Continent would take time. For now, there was a PR war to manage. Damage control. King Henry commissioned Sir Thomas More to lead the propaganda charge against Tyndale and warn his subjects to beware the dreaded texts. Sir More cranked out messages denouncing not only the faulty, heretical wordings in Tyndale's translation but also the fraudulent, hypocritical nature of his character—a man "puffed up with pride and envy." In 1530 More even took the lead in a church council that officially condemned Tyndale's works.

But from his Belgian hideaway of Antwerp, where God had repeatedly allowed the kind, humble Tyndale to slip the noose of those who sought his capture, he wrote a return letter to Sir Thomas More. It included a handful of substantive rebuttals to the slanderous claims against his work, but it had more of a ring of pity to it than provocation.

Tyndale wrote: "Our love and good works do not make God first love us, nor change Him from hate to love. No, His love and deeds make us love, and change us from hate to love. For He loved us when we were evil, when we were His enemies; and chose us to make us good and to show us love and to draw us to Him, that we should love again.

"If you could see what is written in the first epistle of John, though all the other Scriptures were laid apart, you should see all this."

It all came down to love.

But, as the Apostle John had earlier written in quoting the Lord Jesus, "people loved darkness rather than the light." They saw much to gain in holding religious office but little to value in the love of God. They saw even *less* to like in men such as William Tyndale, who threatened their authority by championing Christ's gospel.

So they eventually found him. By a trick (what else?)—a slick-talking spy who took advantage of Tyndale's generous hospitality, and like Judas before him, casually motioned the sheriff's deputies in his direction. For nearly two years Tyndale languished in a cold castle dungeon, shivering from exposure yet sharing the love of God with such genuine courage that even the jailer and his family were won over to Christ.

In the end they would tie him to a post in public view, strangle the last breath from his body, then burn his remains to ashes. The last words from his lips were these: "Lord, open the king of England's eyes."

Let him know the love of God.

WHAT'S YOUR STORY?

How far does the love of God motivate you? Does it truly have a pull on your priorities? Does it carry enough weight to change the way you do business, or treat your family, or spend your money, or invest your Saturdays? What isn't motivated by the love of God is always motivated by love for ourselves. But when gratitude for God's grace is all it takes to make us act, His presence is all it takes to fill us up.

John 15:9-17 • 2 Corinthians 5:14-15 • Titus 2:11-14

JOHN
WESLEY

But to all who did receive Him, He gave them the right to be children of God, to those who believe in His name, who were born, not of blood, or of the will of the flesh, or of the will of man, but of God.

—John 1:12-13

JOHN WESLEY
PERFECT SURRENDER

LONDON, ENGLAND · 1738

If good works could get a person into heaven, John Wesley was one man who could have given the Apostle Paul a really good run for his money.

He had an unbelievable will. A spartan-like level of discipline. The man could not possibly have been more devoted to his prayer and fasting, to reading the Scripture and attending Holy Communion, to visting felons in the jails and giving money that could have been his to London's poor. His pocket diary bulged with accounts of each faithful minute's activity, and any diversion from total self-mastery cut him to the bone. He and the pals he gathered around him at Oxford University even came to be known as "The Holy Club," so devout and determined were they to keep their nose in the Christian classics and their feet in the straight and narrow.

Only one problem. And you've probably already guessed what it was.

Being perfect is a 25-hour-a-day job.

For the perfectionist, there's always more duty than there is daylight, more pressure than there is peace, and always more things to do in order to make God happy. So when John Oglethorpe, member of the House of Commons, put out a call for clergymen who had "contempt of the ornaments and conveniences of life" and who were inclined toward "bodily austerities and serious thoughts," inviting them to set sail to a new colony in America to convert the heathen, guess who was on the first boat to Georgia?

John Wesley left England, ready to save the savages, not yet realizing that there is something savage in all of us. Even the most perfect of us. But a wicked storm worked itself up during the voyage—as they often do in God's impeccable timing. Violent waves climbed higher than the ship, pouring their full power in between the decks, slicing the mainsail into shreds.

The Englishmen on board began screaming in terror.

Who wouldn't?

Well, for one, a little band of German Protestants, better known as Moravians.

Unwilling to let a little high wind interfere with their worship service, they chose to remain calm. In between shrieks and the showers of sea spray, the Moravians could be heard singing their hymns, lifting their prayers, praising their God. The contrast was striking. Striking enough to make John Wesley share his observations the next day with one of their pastors. When he did, the man explained how believers in Christ enjoy the witness of the Holy Spirit in their hearts, how they live in the sure knowledge that they are saved from sin and secured for heaven. "Do *you* know Jesus Christ?" he asked Wesley.

"He that is saved by faith is indeed born again, going on in the might of the Lord his God, from faith to faith, from grace to grace."

"I know He is the Savior of the world." (That wasn't *exactly* what the pastor had asked, was it?)

"True, but do you know He has saved *you*?"

Hmm. Wesley didn't have a straightforward answer to that one, nor did he have much luck during his two-year stint as a soul-winner in the Georgia settlement. His high-church ways and demeanor, his heavy-handed enforcement of rules and regulations, his stubborn refusal to offer Communion to those who weren't truly toeing the line—all these things made his God seem more of a slavemaster than a Savior.

The trip home was hard. The storm had moved inside. "I went to America to convert the Indians, but oh! Who shall convert *me*? Who will deliver me from this evil heart of unbelief?"

The questions lingered for months after his arrival back in London. He knew he needed the faith those Moravian brothers had—not just a faith in God, not just an awareness of His existence, but a kind of belief that released him from the torture of constantly coming up short, never knowing from one day to the next whether God was tickled with his performance or ticked off at his inadequacy.

> "Whatever light you receive [from reading the Scriptures] should be used to the uttermost, and that immediately. So shall you find this word to be indeed the power of God unto present and eternal salvation."

Wesley wanted freedom from his sins, which were eating him alive—and getting harder (not easier) to abstain from. He wanted the kind of joy that could sing through a storm. He wanted the hope of a heavenly future. And he wouldn't mind it, Lord, if faith could feel good once in a while. *Is that something a man can ask You for?*

On May 24, 1738, Wesley awoke to the dawn and his daily appointment with the Scriptures. Strict and methodical as he was, you'd think he would've had a set pattern for his Bible reading. But he was one of those sorts who liked to finger the Book with both hands and flop it open to the first place his eyes would light. On this morning his Testament opened to 2 Peter 1:4: "He has given us very great and precious promises, so that through them you may share in the divine nature, escaping the corruption that is in the world because of evil desires." And then God brought him to the clincher. Wesley glided his thumbs along the rippling page edges, then peeled the leaves apart somewhere in the Gospels. His eye fell on Mark 12:34:

"You are not far from the kingdom of God."

About 16 hours, to be more exact.

A little before 9:00 that night at an evening worship service, he listened as someone read from the preface of Luther's commentary on Paul's letter to the Romans. "While he was describing the change which God works in the heart through faith in Christ"—(where Luther refers to John 1: "to those who believe in His name")—"I felt my heart strangely warmed. I felt that I did trust in Christ, in Christ alone for salvation. And an assurance was given me, that he had taken away my sins, even mine, and saved me from the law of sin and death."

God had given him a saving faith. And my, oh, my—the feeling to go with it!

By 10:00 that evening, he was bursting through the door of his brother Charles' house, a troop of friends in tow, declaring "I believe! I believe!" With hearts ablaze, they sang the roof down with one of Charles' masterful hymns. And the next morning, "the moment I awakened, 'Jesus, Master,' was in my heart and in my mouth. I found that all my strength lay in keeping my eye fixed on Him and my soul waiting on Him continually. Yet the enemy injected a fear: 'If thou dost believe, why is there not a more sensible change?' I answered that I know not. But this I do know—I now have peace with God. And I sin not today, for Jesus my Master has forbidden me to take thought for the morrow.

"Herein I found the difference between this and my former state. I had been striving, fighting with all my might under the law, as well as under grace.

Before, I was sometimes, if not often, conquered. Now, I was always conqueror"—not in his own strength, but in Christ alone.

And such faith would conquer all of England.

Traveling more than 200,000 miles on horseback over the next 50 years "as though he were out of breath in pursuit of souls," he would preach in any field, farmhouse, or forest glade that would give him an audience, sweeping thousands of lives into the Kingdom and setting a spiritual revival in motion that shook England to its roots. Many historians believe that if a man of lesser resolve and character had been the leader of such a movement, Britain would have seen the same sort of upheaval that befell its European neighbors during the French Revolution.

But Wesley, though drawing fire and inciting mobs for shaking up whole cities with his open-air altar calls, never wished to birth an uprising. He simply wanted to announce a new birth, a birth of the heart—"born not of blood, or of the will of the flesh, or of the will of man, but of God."

The God who makes all things perfect.

WHAT'S YOUR STORY?

The most we can ever expect from our human strength is an obedience that performs in spite of inner protests. We're like figure skaters whose high marks for technical difficulty get cancelled out by a painful lack of poise and artistry. Only Christ can turn us wizened sinners into willful followers who do good because we want to, who serve God because we love Him.

Romans 7:1-6 • Galatians 2:15-21 • James 2:8-13

WILLIAM WILBERFORCE

"The tax collector, standing far off, would not even raise his eyes to heaven, but kept striking his chest and saying, 'O God, turn Your wrath from me— a sinner!'"

—Luke 18:13

WILLIAM
WILBERFORCE
THE VOICE OF FREEDOM

LONDON, ENGLAND · 1786

He had one of those voices that made you just want to hear him speak. Today, he'd be all over C-SPAN.

In *his* day he was the rising star of the British Parliament, a young twenty-something bachelor with a smart list of ideas and a smooth way of expressing them. He probably wasn't as cocky as he could have been, but he definitely enjoyed his early life of luxury and legislation. "The first years in Parliament I did nothing—nothing to any purpose. My own distinction was my darling object."

But it wasn't long into his storied career—(is it really long into *anyone's?*)—before the luster had lost its gleam and gloss. Yes, he dined and debated with people of prominence, he socialized with the suave and stylish, he was even best friends with William Pitt, the prime minister—an old acquaintance from college who was now his closest companion in government.

Still, he was dealing with the same questions most everyone asks: What was he really accomplishing with his life? What was the point of what he was doing?

He was also wrestling with a question too *few* people ask (and even *fewer* persist in getting answered): "What shall I do to be saved?"

It was a hard question for a man of his stature to raise. But alone on his bed at night, or in the slow moments of a committee meeting, or amid the pointless conversation of a sophisticated party, the question kept resurfacing—

until he voiced it out loud one late afternoon in a pastor's study on Lombard Street in London.

The man in the chair facing him was John Newton—well-known even then for his dramatic conversion from slave trader to Christian servant and as the writer of hymns like "Amazing Grace." The old churchman listened intently to William's remarkable life story: his brushes with matters of religion, his accomplishments in matters of state, his mighty struggle to see how one life could possibly marry the two. William was becoming aware that the very breath in his body and the eloquent voice that conveyed it, his position in the community and his growing influence in the nation, were every one a loan from God— "a terrible, awe-inspiring trust."

"When I heard someone speak of this man's place, or that man's position, I felt a rising inclination to pursue the same objects, but a Sunday in solitude never failed to restore me to myself."

Didn't God know that underneath the reputation and popularity lived a man so unworthy of such powerful skills?

William Wilberforce knew. And for the first time in his life, he didn't mind admitting it. The words he spoke in the church vestry that grey afternoon had a quality greater than any of the others he had constructed for his "right honorable gentlemen" across the House of Commons. They were full of that trademark sound—clear and passionate, layered with texture and emotion. But he didn't care what it sounded like. Or who heard him say it.

"God . . . be merciful to me . . . a sinner!"

> "Policy is not my principle. There is a principle above everything that is politic, and when I reflect on the command which says: 'Thou shalt do no murder,' how dare I set up any reasonings of my own against it?"

William had found his Savior. And also his calling.

For in that hour of true confession and godly counsel, the voice was joined by a new vision—not just permission to live a public life, but a responsiblity to use it for God's glory. Others who had come to Christ had fled to the outskirts of society, far from taunts and temptation but also isolated from the arenas where God had placed them. Shielded from the hot breath of open hostility, they had been happy to serve God in seclusion. But William was being called to serve God on the stage . . . out in the open where his enemies could take their best shot . . . up in front where his principled policies could make an impact for good on the nation, on the world, on all of mankind.

Looking back on that momentous conversation, John Newton would write, "The joy I felt, and the hopes I conceived, I shall never forget."

William would only remember, "I found my mind in a calm, tranquil state, more humbled, and looking up more devoutly to God."

Christ had put him at peace. Good thing. Because he was about to inherit a storm. For *mercy's* sake.

The cause that would define his life and legacy was first posed to him at a dinner party by a distinguished lady of society. Her interest was in raising awareness and seeking an end to a scourge on England's noble reputation: the slave trade. William wasn't exactly a stranger to the issue. He knew bits and snatches of what went on in the process of acquiring African labor to work the British colonies. He also knew about the vested interests that would oppose any meddling in their money making and property development. He knew he'd have a fight on his hands if he were to put stoppage of the slave trade up for a vote.

As John Wesley would write to him a few days before his own death, "Unless God has raised you up for this very thing, you will be worn out by the opposition of men and devils."

But what's a Christian in public office to do when he begins to peel back the layers of twisted logic supporting a policy like this, and discovers to his horror that underneath lies the bloodied face of wickedness and cruelty? It's enough to make any man of morals recoil in disgust and indignation. It's enough to make a *Christian* man fear the judgment of almighty God.

Innocent men and women were being forced from their homeland, mashed so tightly into slave ships that nearly half failed to survive the heat, stench, and turmoil of the voyage. Those unfortunate enough to endure the trip were stripped naked upon their arrival, branded with a hot iron, yanked from their families, and put to work with little more than a mouthful to eat. The tiniest resistances were met with whips and knives, with melted wax poured boiling hot down their bodies, with salt and pepper smeared over open wounds . . . to make them think twice before it happened again.

You'd think anyone would see that this was insane, barbaric, unbefitting of a world power?

But for eighteen long years William was forced to battle constantly, facing defeat after defeat before his fellow colleagues, baring his back to unabashed personal criticism against "the damnable doctrine of Wilberforce and his hypocritical allies."

"But God will not accept a divided affection. He requires to set up His throne in the heart and to reside in it without a rival. . . . I am here not to gratify my private feelings, but to discharge a great political trust. For the faithful administration of the power vested in me, I must answer to my country, and to God.

"Patriotism is not enough. A man who fears God is not at liberty."

His first victory would finally come in 1807 when both Houses voted for his Abolition of the Slave Trade bill. But it would take many years more before the rule of law could fully enforce his aim. Too many hands were in the till, too many nations benefitting from the barbarism, and it was not until the eve of his death that William was able to hear the news: Slavery had been abolished throughout the entire British Empire.

A final feather in his cap? A just reward for a life of suffering and slander? "I have nothing whatsoever to urge but the poor publican's plea, 'God, be merciful to me, a sinner!' "

That's the voice of freedom talking.

WHAT'S YOUR STORY?

Every one of the stories in this book have proven that God truly speaks through His Word to give ordinary people a power and impact far beyond their own boundaries and abilities. This life is not a dry run. It's the real thing. So if you're ready for God to use what's left of yours for bigger things than you've ever imagined, start getting His Book open every day. And stay in it the rest of your life.

Deuteronomy 30:15-20 • Psalm 119:97-104 • James 1:21-25

CREDITS

The only direct quotes in this book are those ascribed to the featured individuals themselves. But the following books and articles have been very helpful in communicating the historical times and lasting influences of some of these Christian heroes. You might want to look for some of these. Other information has come from general references and public domain sources.

ATHANASIUS
The Story of Christian Theology © 1999 by Roger E. Olson (InterVarsity Press)
The Holy Fire © 1957 by Robert Payne (Harper & Brothers Publishers)

AUGUSTINE
Augustine: Wayward Genius © 1980 by David Bentley-Taylor (Baker Book House)

J.S. BACH
The Bach Reader © 1966 (W.W. Norton & Company)
131 Christians Everyone Should Know © 2000 (Broadman & Holman)
"Bach's Fifth Gospel" © 2000 by Chuck Colson
   (Prison Fellowship Ministries)

CLARA BARTON
Angel of the Battlefield © 1956 by Ishbel Ross (Harper & Row)

DIETRICH BONHOEFFER
Gerhard Leibholz's "Memoir" in *The Cost of Discipleship* © 1959 (SCM Press)
I Knew Dietrich Bonhoeffer © 1966 (Wm. Collins, Sons & Company)

WILLIAM BOOTH
The General Next to God © 1965 by Richard Collier (E.P. Dutton and Company)

DAVID BRAINERD
A Casket of Cameos © 1924 by F. W. Boreham (Abingdon Press)
Flagellant on Horseback © 1950 by Richard Ellsworth Day (Judson Press)

BLAISE PASCAL
Pascal & Fenelon: Devotion in the Age of Enlightenment © 1980
  (Broadman & Holman)

PATRICK OF IRELAND
The Life and Writings of the Historical Saint Patrick
  © 1983 by R. P. C. Hanson (The Seabury Press)

PAUL THE APOSTLE
The Mind of St. Paul © 1958 by William Barclay
  (Harper & Row Publishers)

WILLIAM PENN
A Handful of Stars © 1922 by F.W. Boreham (Abingdon Press)

CHARLES SPURGEON
The Shadow of the Broad Brim © 1934 by Richard Ellsworth Day
  (Judson Press)
"Preaching Through Adversity" © 1995 by John Piper
  (Desiring God Ministries)

CORRIE TEN BOOM
The Hiding Place © 1971 by Corrie ten Boom
  and John and Elizabeth Sherrill (Fleming H. Revell Company)
My Years with Corrie ten Boom ©1978 by Ellen de Kroon Stamps
  (Fleming H. Revell Company)

WILLIAM TYNDALE
From This Verse © 1998 by Robert J. Morgan (Thomas Nelson Publishers)

WILLIAM WILBERFORCE
Sparks Among the Stubble © 1955 by Margaret Cropper
  (Longmans, Green & Company)

If you enjoyed *"Words to Die For,"*
you may want to check out these other B&H titles:

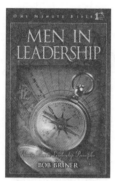

Men in Leadership
0-8054-9153-8

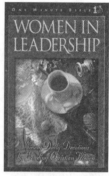

Women in Leadership
0-8054-9193-7

90 Days with the Christian Classics
0-8054-9278-X

Starting Today
0-8054-3780-0